CARDIFF
a city at war

1.   *The Swastika is raised over the City Hall after the Munich Crisis.*

CARDIFF
a city at war

by
Dennis Morgan

1998

Published by
DENNIS MORGAN
139 Carisbrooke Way, Cyncoed,
CARDIFF CF3 7HU

Dedication

To all those people in Cardiff who suffered because of the Second World War.

Published by
DENNIS MORGAN
139 Carisbrooke Way, Cyncoed,
CARDIFF CF3 7HU

ISBN: 0 9534455 0 x

Printed by WBC Book Manuacturers Ltd., Waterton Industrial Estate, Bridgend.
Jacket designed by Eurion Brown, 55 Eastgate, Cowbridge.

Contents

Preface

In this book I have tried to show what life was like for the people of Cardiff during the great conflict which began nearly 60 years ago. One of the problems in studying any theme concerning the Second World War is that of censorship. Contemporary newspaper reports, which I have used a great deal, evoke the atmosphere of the times but the news is often shrouded in secrecy. For example, the activities of enemy agents, detailed reporting about the Blitz, and the Cardiff connection with the St. Nazaire raid and the D-Day preparations, could not be disclosed as long as hostilities lasted.

Fortunately, there are other avenues of research arising from information revealed since 1945. Numerous articles have been written about different aspects of Cardiff at war by Derek Hooper, John O'Sullivan, Dan O'Neill and other contributors in the *South Wales Echo*. In addition, the *Echo* has published a number of war supplements in its *South Wales Yesterday* series and the commemoration of the fiftieth anniversaries of D-Day, VE Day and VJ Day. All these sources not only add to our knowledge but also contain personal anecdotes of the war years. Where I have made use of these, I have tried to offer my thanks personally but, if I have not been able to do so, I am glad to record my appreciation now.

I have made use of the pamphlet, *Bombers Over Wales*, which gives a detailed account of the air raids on Cardiff and was published by the *Western Mail* in 1945. Further information about the Blitz was forthcoming from the interesting booklets compiled by local history groups in Riverside and Llandaff.

I am grateful to the Port Manager at Cardiff for giving me access to the wealth of information relating to the part played by the docks during the war. The minutes of the Cardiff City Council were also enlightening for their insight into the work of the local authority and the role of the emergency services during the crisis.

"Cardiff through the War Years" was an exhibition organised by the Cardiff Heritage Working Party in 1995. I should like to express my appreciation to Mr. Matthew Williams, who co-ordinated the display, for giving me access to the material used at that time. In particular, I would like to thank those people who have allowed me to interview them about their wartime experiences. Their names are mentioned throughout the book and their reminiscences add both detail and colour to this story.

Once again I have received invaluable support from Mr. Bryn Jones and his colleagues in the Local Studies Department of the Cardiff Central Library. They were most helpful in assisting me during my research. I must also acknowledge the excellent work of Mr. Eurion Brown of Keith Brown & Sons Ltd.,

Cowbridge, and Mr. Peter Tremewen and the staff of WBC Book Manufacturers, Bridgend in ensuring the smooth transition of this book into print. Friendly advice was also given to me by Mr. Stewart Williams on matters relating to the publishing business. Mr. Dennis Pope, as usual, has processed my photographs in a most professional manner.

I am always grateful for the inspiration, practical help and encouragement I am given by all my family. Despite pressures of work, Ian has kept my brain tuned to the eccentricities of computer technology, while Val and Kathryn have made several useful suggestions in taking on the task of checking the text.

It is customary for the author to take responsibility and apologise in advance for any errors and flaws contained in the book. I am aware that these are more likely than usual in a work which relies upon living memory to a great extent. Having said that, I hope the book will be seen as a tribute to those people in our city who lived and died in the most tumultuous years of this century.

Acknowledgement of photographic sources

My photographs came from several quarters and help to conjure up a vivid portrayal of a city at war. Many of them originate from the *Western Mail* and *South Wales Echo* and I am grateful for the permission I was given to use them. Associated British Ports, the Cardiff City Council and the Cardiff Central Library were also major contributors to whom I am indebted. Other illustrations have been supplied by the following people and organisations: AWE, Albert Barnes, Ted Chamberlain, Bob Chappell, Phyllis Condon, Edward Curran & Co., Elizabeth Dart, John F. David, Drusilla Elliott, Margaret Ellis, Anthony Fisher, Victor Hardacre, M.N. Heard, Reg Hoskins, K. Hubbard, Imperial War Museum, IWM, Lyndon Jewkes, Fred Jones, Malcolm Jones, Steve Jones, Margaret Leonard, Jack Matthews, *News of the World*, Dennis Pope, Fred Stansfield, Terry Sylvester, A.G. Taylor, Yvonne Thomas, Aubrey Waters, John and Eileen Watts, Howard Wiggins, Matthew Williams and Stewart Williams. I would like to thank them all and apologise if I have inadvertently omitted anyone.

List of Illustrations

Chapter One

The Phoney War

An Uneasy Peace

When Neville Chamberlain informed the British people on 3 September 1939 that Hitler had ignored his government's ultimatum, and that "consequently this country is at war with Germany", it came as no surprise. Despite a reluctance to face the horrible possibility of war, portents of the coming conflict had been apparent for years. Since 1933 Jewish refugees from Germany had sought shelter in Britain, bringing with them tales of the dark night descending on their country. Many of them settled in Cardiff though not all Germans living in the city at that time were victims of Nazi persecution. There were some who took advantage of British hospitality to ferret out information which would be useful in the event of war.

The Flottmann Drill Company, now the site of Britton's Building Supplies in Allensbank Road, was the British subsidiary of a German firm. Its managing director was Hans Kuhnemann whose activities have been researched by John O'Sullivan and chronicled in several articles for the *South Wales Echo*. Kuhnemann was a fanatical Nazi who was planted by German intelligence to gather military and industrial information in South Wales. Tall, arrogant and sporting a monocle, this former Prussian Guards officer made little effort to hide his light under a bushel. The walls of his office in Allensbank Road were adorned with pictures of Hitler and Ribbentrop, Germany's ambassador to Britain. He was also the leading light at Anglo-German nights in the Park Hotel, where the Fuhrer's health was toasted before the glasses were thrown into the fireplace. Not unnaturally, this flamboyant gesture angered the manager enough to put an end to such meetings.

Kuhnemann travelled widely in South Wales and the Midlands and during these excursions he practised his skills as a keen photographer. His photographs, many of them taken in the course of pleasure flights from Pengam Airport, were supplemented with postcards. On the outbreak of war, these illustrations were incorporated into aerial guide books and proved to be an invaluable aid to the Luftwaffe when the blitz on Cardiff was launched. In peaceful pre-war Britain, though the authorities were well aware of Kuhnemann's spying activities, no restrictions were placed on his movements. It was not until 3 September that detectives from Special Branch at last paid a visit to him at his home in

GB **7**, BB 32, Nr. 85: Queen Alexandra Dock im Hafen von Cardiff (Glamorganshire).
...en Alexandra Dock mit Tankanlagen und Pumpwerk (Schornstein, rechts vorn). Rechte Längsseite: Bekohlung...
Langsseite: Kuhlhaus und Lagerhauser. Hintere Querseite: Holzlagerplatz und Brikettfabrik (Schornstein)...
...n rechts: Roath Dock, links davon (Mitte) das kleine Roath Basin mit Durchfahrt nach hinten (Mitte)...
...zum langen Bute East Dock, daneben links das schmale Bute West-Dock

2.   *A photograph of the Cardiff Docks issued to German airmen.*

Marlborough Road. They were too late. Kuhnemann and his wife had departed from Cardiff a few days earlier and, after helping to burn documents at the German Embassy, made their escape before war was declared.

Kuhnemann was not the only German in Cardiff with Nazi sympathies. Dr. Friedrich Schoberth was a senior lecturer in German at University College. During the war he edited the scripts of William Joyce, the notorious "Lord Haw-Haw", who lived in Colum Road for a time in the 1930s. In his propaganda broadcasts from Germany, Lord Haw-Haw added a little local colour drawn from his knowledge of South Wales. "The dial at the back of the Town Hall clock in Barry is a minute faster than the one overlooking King's Square", seems an innocent enough remark. Yet comments of this kind added credibility to more insidious propaganda such as the sinking of the *Ark Royal* which Joyce announced at least 10 times before it really happened. Likewise, in a broadcast to British forces serving overseas in January 1941, he tried to undermine the morale of men from Cardiff by telling them that that their Civic Centre had been razed to the ground.

Kuhnemann and Schoberth outlived the war and Kuhnemann even tried to return to Cardiff but, if he had any friends in the city, they were not prepared to welcome him back. William Joyce was captured in 1945 and, after a trial at the Old Bailey, was hanged as a traitor a year later.

The German threat to invade Czechoslovakia in September 1938 was an omen of the ordeal soon to come. The *Western Mail* reported "Prayers for Peace", as Neville Chamberlain negotiated with Hitler in an attempt to prevent the crisis leading to war. The gloom deepened as hostilities seemed imminent and the fear of bombardment from the air intensified. Sandbags surrounded the City Hall and other public buildings. A thousand stretchers were ordered as plans were made to

3.   *Trenches being dug in Cathays Park in September 1938.*

evacuate children and turn the infant departments into first aid posts. Gas masks were hurriedly assembled and arrangements made to collect them from schools throughout the city. Long queues formed at each centre as volunteer air raid wardens distributed the respirators in brown paper bags. Later, the bags were replaced with cardboard cartons which could be slung over the shoulder. It was the first sign of events to come and a teacher at Howard Gardens High School remembers arriving there, "to find soldiers at the school gates and our hall stacked high with cases containing gas masks. This was our first contact with war, though only a threat in this case".

Few people at this time had any kind of air raid shelter. Corporation employees and men drawn from the ranks of the unemployed were hurriedly assembled to dig 9 miles of trenches in Cathays Park, Sophia Gardens and other open spaces around the city. These trenches, covered with corrugated iron sheets, only provided shelter for 10% of the population in the most crowded areas of the city and were hardly an adequate shield against enemy bombers.

Then Chamberlain made his dramatic visit to Munich and returned with a promise of "peace in our time". The *South Wales Echo* hailed the "Great News" and reported how, "people dashed about waving their newspapers and shouting there isn't going to be any war". The Cardiff Business Club saluted the Prime Minister as "World Peacemaker Number One". The Lord Mayor gave orders that the flags of all the nations, participating in the Munich agreement, should be flown from the City Hall. Among these of course was the Swastika and some councillors were so incensed by its appearance that they forcibly removed it. The Lord Mayor's claim, that he "would not insult anyone by omitting their flag", cut little ice with the majority of people who agreed with Arthur Horner, the South

Wales miners' leader, that the incident was, "a disgrace to the whole Welsh community".

At the time, the public reaction was an overwhelming sense of relief, a view which was epitomised by the offer in the *Western Mail* of a commemorative plate, dedicated to Mr. and Mrs. Chamberlain, "A picture you will want to frame, to hang in your house and treasure for ever". Yet significantly the editorial in the *Western Mail* on the same day reflected that, "time alone can show whether Hitler's appetite for conquest has been satisfied".

The winter passed uneasily as people pondered whether Hitler could be trusted. The distribution of gas masks continued but the trenches dug the previous autumn, apart from those in Sophia Gardens, were filled in because of their waterlogged and dangerous condition. In February the ARP Committee ordered the City Engineer to proceed with plans to provide 220 public shelters. Basements in many buildings were strengthened to offer protection to the community and it was at this time that the walls of Cardiff Castle were earmarked for a purpose the Romans had never intended. A ramp from Duke Street, now replaced with a glass window, led to a solid shelter for more than 2,500 people. There were only cold, stone slabs to sit on but, when the blitz began, people were glad to seek the protective shield of these walls.

Soon afterwards shelters were distributed to those houses which had a garden. They were named after the Home Secretary, Sir John Anderson, and were free to households with an annual income of less than £250 a year. For those who were more affluent a charge of £10 was levied. By July 1940 there were enough shelters of one kind or another to accommodate 155,000 people, a remarkable achievement in such a short time. Unfortunately, the public shelters were often

4.   *The Air Raid Shelter at Cardiff Castle.*

5.   *Rhiwbina pupils with their gas masks 1939.*

abused and vandalised, despite regular use of disinfectant and the efforts of the police to catch the perpetrators.

In March 1939 Hitler occupied the rest of Czechoslovakia, dashing the false hopes raised at Munich. Soon afterwards Britain gave its fateful guarantee to aid Poland in the event of a German invasion and the Conscription Act passed through its final stages in Parliament. April 26 was the last opportunity for men to volunteer for military service as an alternative to conscription, and that day the Teritorial Army Office in Queen Street worked a 24 hour shift to deal with a last minute rush of 200 volunteers.

The deepening gloom was reflected in Neville Chamberlain's visit to Cardiff in June. Gone was the optimistic theme of "Peace in our time". Instead he spoke of Britain's powerful navy and an air force, growing "at a rate beyond our expectation". In August, the Government announced its plans to repair houses and deal with the homeless in the event of war. A foretaste of things to come took place on 19 August when Cardiff was chosen as one of 6 British cities to be "attacked" by French aircraft. The exercise was intended both to assess the response of Fighter Command and also to give practice to the Civil Defence forces.

A few days later the National Museum of Wales closed its doors to the public as its most valuable treasures were stored in purpose-built strongrooms. It re-opened a month later and continued to function throughout the war, despite a depleted staff and fewer exhibits. At the City Hall, workmen began to brick up the windows of the Marble Hall so that its statues of famous Welshmen could be protected.

The waiting was over on Friday 1 September when Germany attacked Poland and the faint hope of avoiding hostilities disappeared. The evacuation of children was already under way and last minute checks were made to ensure that gas masks were in working order. People were warned to take these respirators everywhere and, if the gas rattle sounded, "to put them on at once, even in bed". For a month or two, everyone heeded the Government warning but, as both sides observed a truce in the use of gas warfare, the number of people carrying their masks became fewer and fewer.

There was a strange paradox about that last weekend of peace. Thousands of men were on their way to Territorial Army camps, while Cardiff City were losing 4-2 to Notts County at Ninian Park before a crowd of 20,000. It was to be their last football league match for 7 years. At Barry Island, as children still played on the beach, troops were filling sandbags. Once war was declared, air raids were expected immediately and the sandbags would be needed, both to protect public buildings and hospitals, and to give the general public the means of dealing quickly with incendiary bombs. When Britain's ultimatum to Germany expired at 11 o'clock on Sunday 3 September, the streets were almost deserted as people sadly awaited the inevitable outcome. Many people were in church and services were interrupted to inform them of the Prime Minister's announcement that Britain was at war for the second time in 25 years.

Calm Before the Storm

The anticipated air attacks did not happen, at least for the moment, though Ted Chamberlain of Llanishen remembers diving for cover when a squadron of planes flew over the village. Fortunately, they proved to be aircraft from St. Athan on a training flight. Schools were shut for a week and the fear of air raids led to the temporary closure of crowded premises, such as sports arenas, cinemas and theatres. For several months the whole country entered into a period nicknamed by the Americans as the "Phoney War". The nation was at war with Germany but, except at sea, very little fighting took place between the adversaries.

Blackout restrictions were imposed from 1 September 1939 and for 5 years every window had to be covered with dark material. In addition, it was prudent to put sticky tape across all windows to offset the effects of flying splinters of glass from an explosion. Even the smallest chink of light had to be hidden, as there was a popular belief that it could be seen from 10,000 feet in the air and fitting blackout curtains to bay windows was a particular problem in view of their shape The regulations were quite draconian in their application and, on one occasion during the blitz, an officer in the Home Guard was fined 10/6d★ because the

★In this book, all references to the currency are quoted in pre-decimal coinage. For the benefit of younger readers, one shilling (1/-) or 12d represents 5p, while 20 shillings (20/-) are the equivalent of £1 (100p). As an example, 10 shillings is equal to 50p and 35/- is equal to £1.75. The average wage in the war years was £5 to £6 a week so, to have an idea of wages, prices or fines in present day terms, you would have to multiply by 50 or 60.

6.   *A white line marks the middle of Newport Road in the blackout.*

glow of his cigarette was visible while an air raid was in progress. A much more severe punishment was imposed on a man in Wellington Street, who was sentenced to 7 weeks imprisonment for using obscene language to a female air raid warden after she had warned him about breaching the lighting restrictions.

As a further step to thwart marauding aircraft, all vehicle lights were restricted to a narrow slit, while tram and bus windows were blacked out with a dark blue paint. The *Western Mail* warned passengers who had scratched the paint in an effort to see where they were going, "This must not be done under any circumstances". When coal was being fed into the furnace of a railway engine, open spaces were covered with a canvas hood so that the flames could not be seen from the sky.

Street lighting of course virtually disappeared and in the early days there were accidents because motorists hugged the white lines in the middle of the road. In fact, during that first winter of the war, more deaths occurred in the blackout than from enemy action. By January 1940, it was estimated that one person in five had been injured in such accidents as walking into lamp posts or stumbling over kerbs. At Winston Churchill's suggestion, very dim lighting was restored at cross roads and other danger spots. The use of torches in the blackout was also permitted, as long as they were pointed downwards and masked with 2 layers of tissue paper. Even so, several people were prosecuted for shining their torches too conspicuously in an attempt to find their way in the dark.

George Pritchard, a pensioner aged 74, became an early victim of the new regulations when he was knocked down by a taxi in St. Mary Street on 2 September. He died at the City Lodge the next day. Driving became slightly more easy when buses and cars were given a daub of white paint on their mudguards,

7.   *Trees, kerbs and lamp posts are given a coat of white paint in Grand Avenue.*

while kerbs, trees and lamp posts were similarly decorated to help people find their way in the dark.

Perhaps the most absurd comment about the blackout came from a *Western Mail* reader who criticised housewives for leaving their washing out at night, arguing that a few white garments would inform enemy pilots they were over a town. A rather more serious incident involved a neutral ship sailing into Cardiff. It was lit sufficiently to show its flag of neutrality but was fired upon by troops stationed at Lavernock. The captain protested but was told in no uncertain terms that the light could be a means of guiding enemy aircraft into Cardiff Docks. Night work at the port was very dangerous. The only illumination was the whitewash on the coping stones and, in the early years of the war, many dockers lost their lives through accidents. Eventually safety measures were improved and the casualty rate fell by 90%.

Margaret Booth, now Mrs. Leonard, kept a diary during the war and recalls the first blackout vividly. "I had gone to the Park Hall cinema with my brother. When we came out, the street lamps were not lit as usual and our tram had its windows blacked out. We got off at the bottom of Penylan Hill and there I saw a soldier with his rifle and all his kit. He was a Territorial on his way to the station and it brought home to me that war was imminent".

It was claimed that the only beneficiaries of the blackout were courting couples and burglars, though there were also complaints about unscrupulous shopkeepers who refused to sell blackout materials and drawing pins unless customers bought other goods as well. The Lord Mayor of Cardiff suggested that such cases should be reported to the appropriate authorities but the Mayor of Newport went further and threatened to name all such profiteers in the local press.

The Registry Office in Cardiff remained open on Sunday 3 September, and there was a flurry of activity as couples brought the date of their wedding forward before the men were called to their regiments. Cardiff's first war bride was Nancy Thomas who married Thomas Owen Tims after morning service at St. Andrews Church. A few days later Maurice Turnbull, the Glamorgan cricket captain, married Elizabeth Rowley Brooke at Scunthorpe before taking up active service. A year later their daughter was born but their marriage, as for so many others, would end in tragedy because of the war.

All police leave was suspended at the outbreak of hostilities. A 24-hour police guard was placed on vital installations such as Wood Street Railway Bridge, power stations, gas works and the BBC Studios in Park Place. There were Germans among the crews of some of the ships in Cardiff Docks and they were arrested. Many of them seemed quite happy to be escaping from the coming conflict.

The Government assumed the right to requisition any item needed for war service. Frank Gaccon, commander of the Auxiliary Fire Service in Cardiff, had converted an ex-naval pinnace into a superb sea-going cruiser before the war. The *Lady Drusie*, named after his daughter, Drusilla, was his pride and joy but it was now commandeered for mine-sweeping duties. Sadly, it was sunk with the loss of 8 lives when it struck a mine in the Bristol Channel in November 1940.

For the moment Cardiff, like the rest of Britain, showed few signs of a nation at war. Petrol was rationed from 22 September, but food rationing was only gradually introduced the following January and meat rationing did not begin until March. People with money to spare ignored the warnings about hoarding food, and stocked up with tinned goods and non-perishable items during this period before rationing began. At this stage there were no queues and "plenty for

8. *Barrage balloons in Cathays Park 1940.*

all" was the optimistic comment from the Ministry of Food. It would be some time before shortages became apparent, though Howell's store advertised galvanised buckets, suitable for sand or water, and warned the public, "Now is the time to replenish your china cupboard while stocks last".

Only the barrage balloons flying over the city suggested that times were no longer normal. Early in 1939 the Air Ministry had purchased 31 acres of land at Caerau as a barrage for 24 balloons, though Lord Haw-Haw later tried to convince the people of Cardiff that only 7 of these monsters had been allocated for their protection. The balloons remained a part of Britain's defences until 1943 and were intended to prevent low flying aircraft from bombing accurately. Any open space could be used as a convenient site and they were soon accepted as part of the normal scenery at the docks or in Cathays Park, Ely Racecourse and many of Cardiff's recreation grounds. Even a small park, such as Pentre Gardens in Grangetown, was large enough to accommodate a single balloon and the lorry to which it was attached. Its crew slept in St. Samson's church hall and found a friendly welcome among the local people who were prepared to offer them a hot bath or even an invitation to dinner.

Teams of 10 men or 16 women were needed to handle these bulky objects which sometimes ran amok. In the first winter of the war, great excitement occurred when one of the balloons broke free of its moorings and created a trail of destruction along a Cardiff street. Chimney pots and lamp posts were ripped from their moorings and news of the rogue monster was hastily transmitted to Balloon Command's headquarters at Ely, where the Western Leisure Centre now stands. From there a fighter plane was summoned to shoot it down and prevent further damage. In another incident, a balloon was hovering over the castle when

9.   These balloon hangars at Caerau were still there in the 1960s.

10. *Christmas as usual 1939.*

11.   The frozen Glamorganshire Canal at Gabalfa in the winter of 1940.

it was struck by lightning and fell to earth in flames, with its cables draped across the nearby streets.

Only on the high seas, where the Battle of the Atlantic began on the very first day, was the war raging in earnest. Merchant ships came under attack from U-boats and surface raiders. The pocket battleship *Graf Spee* was the most formidable of these predators. Eric Elcock from Whitchurch was third engineer on the SS *Trevanion* when it was sunk by the *Graf Spee* on 22 October. He was taken prisoner and later transferred to the German supply vessel, *Altmark*. Elcock only remained a prisoner until February 1940. The *Altmark* was lying in neutral Norwegian waters when the prisoners became aware of the presence of a British destroyer. They made a deafening clamour and, as the *Altmark* was boarded by British sailors, Eric Elcock said, "I have never seen a more thankful lot of men than those of us who went on board the destroyer that night". For the first time he heard the story of how the *Graf Spee* had been scuttled by its captain in Montevideo the previous December.

The first Christmas of the war seemed little different from those of previous years. Most families still had a stock of pre-war luxuries into which they were able to dip for the last time. Lewis Hawes in the *Western Mail* wrote, "Banish the thought, all you war pessimists, that this Christmas is going to be a dull one". Of the thousands of toys in one store, a best seller was an elaborate version of the "impregnable" Maginot line. Godfrey's music shop was advertising its new pianos with the unlikely observation, "Everyone is saying we must have a new piano for Christmas". Ashton's in the Market and James Cox in Queen Street were taking orders as usual for poultry, while an advertisement for Merrett's Christmas cakes promised they would be as rich and fruity as ever. On Boxing Day, a crowd of 12,000 turned up to watch Cardiff City lose 5-2 to Wolverhampton Wanderers.

There were the usual Christmas parties. The Cardiff Missions to Seamen presented its guests with gifts of cigarettes, tobacco, chocolates and the choice of a knitted helmet, gloves or socks. Fathers and sons may have been absent from many homes but the Salvation Army in Adamsdown gave its annual children's party. The youngsters devoured a tea of bread and butter, cakes and jellies that would be a happy memory during the years of austerity that lay ahead. They also took home with them a bag of sweets, a small gift and an orange.

Early in 1940, the principal topic of conversation was the weather as Britain shivered in the worst winter since 1895. The Severn was partly covered in ice and in some places there were snow drifts as high as 12 feet. Electricity was cut off, telegraph poles were down and coal exports at the docks came to a standstill as lifting gear was frozen solid. Details of the great freeze were not released in the press until a fortnight later, as such information might be of value to the enemy who was almost certainly suffering from the same Arctic conditions.

So the war drifted along. Easter Monday 1940 saw good crowds at Barry Island where the fairground and the shops opened for the summer season. The Government promised that nothing would be done, "to hamper the freedom of holiday resorts" and the steady flow of traffic to Barry suggested that petrol rationing was not yet causing any hardship. There was some regret that the Welsh Grand National would not be run at Ely Racecourse on Easter Tuesday but other sports continued to flourish. Two weeks earlier, a crowd of 40,000 had watched England defeat Wales 18-9 at the Arms Park. A complacent Neville Chamberlain informed the nation, "One thing is certain. Hitler has missed the bus". The Fuhrer's reply was to invade Denmark and Norway a week later. The phoney war was over and reality was about to dawn.

Chapter Two

At Bay

Dunkirk

The invasion of Denmark and Norway was merely Hitler's opening gambit. On 10 May 1940, the same day that Winston Churchill replaced Neville Chamberlain as Prime Minister, the German army attacked the Low Countries. J.C. Walker's cartoon that day shows Hitler parachuting on to the bayonets of the Allies, an optimistic point of view as events were soon to show. Within a few days the grim truth emerged. "Nazis rain death on open town" and "Refugees gunned from the air", were the headlines as the *South Wales Echo* reflected more accurately the reality of total war.

As the Wehrmacht stormed through Holland, Belgium and France, refugees sought sanctuary in this country and Cardiff was chosen as one of the reception areas for them. On 21 May more than 100 refugees, whose ages ranged from a child just a few months old to a white-haired old lady of 80, arrived in the city. They had escaped in fishing boats from Ostend, "where the whole harbour was ablaze", and embarked on a hazardous journey which had taken 8 days to complete. Some of them could remember staying in Cardiff as refugees during the First World War and one had been born in the city at that time. Another was adamant that being forced to flee from his native land a second time was enough and he was never going back.

Eventually more than 500 Dutch and Belgian refugees were accommodated in Cardiff. Temporary shelter was found for them in the schoolroom of Roath Road Church and at the Presbyterian Church House in Windsor Place. Later they were accommodated in empty houses or billeted with families who volunteered to take them in. The Government made an allowance of £1 a week for adult refugees and 35/- for a couple. Henry Johns, Lord Mayor of Cardiff, appealed to the citizens of Cardiff to support a fund "for these victims of Nazi ruthlessness". The public responded generously and gifts of essential furniture, bedding, children's toys, clothing and money were handed in to the WVS in St. Mary Street.

Then came the epic of Dunkirk. Tom Flavin from Corporation Road in Cardiff was among the 338,000 men evacuated from those bloodstained beaches. After being wounded in the Battle of Flanders, a mate came to his aid and carried him on a bicycle to Dunkirk. For two days he lay on the beach, constantly

12. *J.C.Walker in optimistic mood, 10 May 1940.*

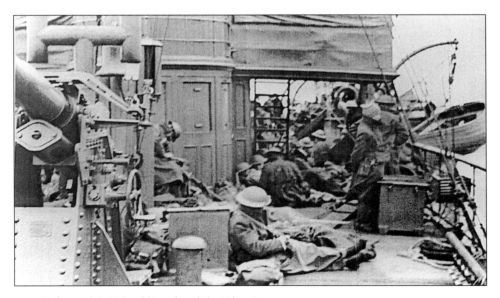

13. *Exhausted British soldiers aboard the Glen Avon.*

14.   Homeward bound on the Glen Avon.

bombarded by the Luftwaffe, before he was rescued. Dead men, still clutching their rifles, lay among the living. In later years Tom recalled how a British pilot was machine gunned by the enemy as he bailed out of his aircraft and, when a German prisoner found this spectacle amusing, a British officer shot him dead. One of the most incongruous sights on that beach were the thousands of packets of cigarettes and bottles of whisky floating in the water, dumped there by the NAAFI to prevent them falling into German hands.

Another hero was Flying Officer Billy New of Whitchurch Road. He was shot down over the Channel during the evacuation and swam for 3 miles before a minesweeper spotted him and threw him a rope. Before Billy could get aboard, the vessel was attacked from the air and was forced to take evasive action, towing the airman along in its wake. Eventually the German bomber was driven off and Billy New was finally hauled aboard.

Dunkirk will always be remembered as the saga of the little ships. Vessels of every description set sail for the French port, running the gauntlet of enemy aircraft in a desperate race against time to bring home the trapped British army. Joining this armada were Campbell's paddle steamers which, in more peaceful times, had given so much pleasure to holiday makers with their day trips to Weston, Minehead or Ilfracombe. At the outbreak of war, these vessels were commandeered as minesweepers. At Bristol, Penarth and the Mountstuart Dry Dock in Cardiff, they were refitted for war duties with a lick of grey paint and the protection of a 12-pounder gun. For 8 months the Campbell's steamers swept for mines in the North Sea from the Firth of Forth to the Tyne. Then, towards the end of May, eight of them were given a signal to return to port. They were given extra ammunition and ordered to proceed at once to Dunkirk. As they raced along at full speed, flames more than 20 feet high erupted from their funnels. Navigation was a simple matter of merely following the armada of barges, lifeboats, coasters and river boats making their way across the English Channel to Dunkirk.

Their shallow draught allowed the paddle steamers to move in close to the shore but the *Glen Gower* went aground under the weight of extra fuel and ammunition. Undeterred, her crew rowed boats to the shore to pick up the waiting soldiers. These boats were designed to carry 26 people but, despite constant machine gunning from the air, most of them carried twice that number with many of the soldiers clinging desperately to the sides. Meanwhile the *Snaefell,* the new name given to the *Waverley*, pulled the *Glen Gower* away from the sand bank but the troubles of the gallant little vessel were not yet over. Ten soldiers were killed as the ship was hit by a shell but undaunted the crew continued to pick up troops until eventually there were 1,500 men on board.

As the vessel set sail for Harwich, it passed the grim spectacle of a funnel sticking out of the water. It was the only visible part of its sister ship, the *Brighton Belle*, which had sunk after striking a submerged wreck. The following Sunday a poem, written by Beverley Nichols of the *Sunday Chronicle*, paid tribute to the unlucky pleasure steamer:

> "Any more for the *Brighton Belle*,
> Come on chum, we're on our way
> Bearing the lads who fought and fell,
> Out of this hell of shot and shell,
> Jerry must wait till another day.
> Any more? Any more?
> Any more for the *Brighton Belle*?"

As it steamed into Harwich, the flag of the *Glen Gower* was at half mast for the fallen. After being re-fuelled and patched up the ship set off once more for Dunkirk. This time it was dark. There were sunken vessels everywhere but another 700 men were taken aboard. Some of them still had their bren guns which they lashed to the rails as a puny protection against the attacks from the air. Three times in all *Glen Gower* made that hazardous voyage, bringing home more than 3,000 men.

Apart from the *Brighton Belle*, Campbell's fleet also lost the *Devonia* and its sister ship, the *Brighton Queen*. After bomb damage to its stern the *Devonia* was deliberately beached at La Panne so that it could be used as a boarding point for the troops. Ninian O'Brien of Daisy Street was a cook on the *Brighton Queen* and he explained to a *Western Mail* reporter how the ship was attacked by 2 dive

15. *The sinking of the Brighton Belle.*

16.   Glen Gower in happier times

bombers and sank in less than three minutes. Miraculously, 200 sailors and soldiers were saved.

The *Glen Avon* completed 2 crossings to bring troops off the beaches at La Panne. Later in the war, the ship was converted into an anti-aircraft vessel and was given a communications role during the landings on D-Day. In September 1944 it foundered off the beaches of Normandy during a severe storm. The *Snaefell,* having rescued 981 men at Dunkirk, resumed its minesweeping duties until it was sunk off West Hartlepool in 1941 by enemy bombers. Sadly the *Glen Gower,* together with the other survivors of Campbell's steamers, ended their days at the scrapyard. In June 1940 J.B. Priestley paid this moving tribute to the little ships which had performed such heroic deeds at Dunkirk: "Our great-grandchildren when they learn how we began this war by snatching glory out of defeat and then swept on to victory, may also learn how the little holiday steamers made an excursion to hell and came back glorious".

As troop trains began to arrive in Cardiff, the weary soldiers were met by the WVS with hot meals and drinks. After their experiences in Belgium, interviewers were regarded with suspicion and one reporter was bluntly asked, "How do I know you're from the *Western Mail*?" Arrangements were made to quarter the troops at Maindy Barracks or in empty houses nearby and a military camp, which would later be used as a base for American soldiers, was hastily constructed on Heath Park. The survivors of Dunkirk wore a mixture of outfits. One man had the boots of a German parachutist while another had acquired a rather gaudy uniform from a French officer. Unshaven and unkempt as they were, the residents of Cathays took these men to their hearts, sharing in the spirit of deliverance that swept the nation. They were offered a meal, cigarettes, sweets and, perhaps most important of all, a hot bath before they reported to their units once more. The *Echo* reported that all the soldiers, despite their weary, battle-stained appearance, still had a smile of appreciation for their warm welcome. Some even forgot their ordeal for the moment to comment on the "cleanliness and beauty of Cardiff . . . and a people whose generosity and warm hospitality would never be forgotten".

17.   *Return from Dunkirk.*

The Home Guard

After Dunkirk, as Churchill was to reflect in later years, "There was a white glow, overpowering, sublime, which ran through our Island from end to end". The miraculous rescue of the BEF was a reason for thanksgiving but, coupled with it, was the knowledge that the invasion of our island for the first time in 900 years was now a possibility. All the lethargy which had characterised the Chamberlain Government disappeared and the nation bonded together in the face of common danger. The "Dunkirk spirit" was based, not on blind ignorance of Britain's perilous plight, but on a sense of realism. As I was told in one interview, "I half wished it would end but I was terrified at the thought of surrender. There seemed no alternative but to just keep going".

Anthony Eden, the Secretary of State for War, launched an appeal on 14 May calling on men, aged between 17 and 65, to join the Local Defence Volunteers. Later, at the suggestion of Winston Churchill, the LDV became the Home Guard. Before Eden had finished his speech, local police stations were inundated with a flood of volunteers. Some of them, recruited from large organisations such as the Guest Keen Works, the National Museum and departments of the City Council, were formed into works battalions. Others, coming from every walk of life, joined their local group.

The comedy series, *Dad's Army*, suggests that the recruits were a motley crew and to some extent this was true. Among the volunteers in Llantwit Major was a 63 year old Zulu, whose eligibility to enlist was questioned because his father had fought against the British at Rorke's Drift. He was recruited, possibly as some implied, because the Germans would assume they had made a serious navigational error if they encountered him after landing along the South Wales coast.

A fund of humorous stories surrounds the activities of the Home Guard nor

18.   Recruits for the Home Guard on parade at Cardiff Arms Park.

were leaders like Captain Mainwaring unknown. An officer, who was a shop manager in his full-time occupation, thought it would be a morale boosting exercise to ford the River Ely at Leckwith when it was in full flood. His platoon contained a number of men who had fought in the trenches of the First World War. On Sunday morning everyone was present when their commanding officer told them of his great idea. One of the veterans called out, "We're right behind you, Sir. Lead the way". The Captain looked hard at the surging torrent and hastily said: "Well! Perhaps we'll save it for another day".

A unit drawn from a Cardiff brewery disgraced itself on one occasion when it was due for inspection by a visiting general. The men had several drinks before they began their march. As they approached the toilets on Cardiff Bridge, nature had to take its course and there was a mad dash for the lavatories. The bewildered general saluted the few stalwarts still marching in step while the rest of the platoon raced along the pavement trying to catch them up.

A more serious incident occurred when the Home Guard at Penarth was manning a rocket launcher. As an aeroplane passed overhead the air raid siren sounded the alert. The unit's orders were to "stand fast" but one team was so keyed up that they fired their rockets. A Wellington bomber was forced to make an emergency landing with an American officer on board. No-one was hurt but the culprits were never allowed to forget how they had forced down one of their own aircraft.

After the losses at Dunkirk, weapons were in such short supply that the volunteers had to find their own. The Earl of Plymouth, as Lord Lieutenant, launched an appeal for shotguns, sporting rifles and pistols for the Home Guard. Any of these was a real prize and it was more common for early drill exercises to be carried out with broom sticks serving as rifles. Sometimes the only weapon available was a bludgeon made from an old golf club or even a packet of pepper to throw in the face of an unwelcome visitor. Training exercises often took on a

19. *Home Guard in training near Cardiff.*

bizarre element. I can remember playing "Cowboys and Indians" in the Plymouth Woods, when the Home Guard arrived and sent us packing before they began what seemed a similar game.

Despite such tales, which have passed into folklore, the Home Guard became an efficient force, especially when they were issued with proper weapons. Later in the war, the Ely unit held shooting contests with American servicemen and never lost a match. By 1943 the average age of the Home Guard had been reduced to 29 and the introduction of conscription emphasised the importance of their role. Any member, who did not take his duties seriously, was fined as a man from Caerphilly was to discover. He joined the Home Guard in 1940 but, when it seemed the danger of invasion had passed, he failed to turn up on parade for six months. He was given the option of a £20 fine or a month in jail.

This kind of behaviour was unusual. Most volunteers in the Home Guard were prepared to sacrifice family life and spend long hours on duty, carrying out essential tasks which otherwise would have fallen on the regular army. Alfred Colley, engaged in essential work as a head shunter at the Newtown marshalling yard, was not required for military service. So he joined the Home Guard and at weekends was taught by regular soldiers how to fire a rifle, throw a hand grenade and man one of the anti–aircraft guns at Lavernock Point or Ely Racecourse. In addition, one night a week was spent on guard duty, either at Queen Street Station or at the Racecourse. Arriving home at 5 a.m., Alf often had to make a quick change of clothing to commence his shift on the railway an hour later. The Home Guard was also trained in fire fighting and one night an incendiary bomb caused a conflagration in the refreshment rooms at the station. Alf and his colleagues received a commendation for the speedy manner in which they quenched the flames. Looking back, Mr. Colley says, "It was a seven day week with perhaps eight hours rest at weekends. I often wonder where we got the

20.   *Llanishen and Lisvane Home Guard platoon at Plas-y-Delyn 1940.*

21. Civil Defence on duty in Mill Lane during the training exercise of October 1941.

stamina to do all these things, taking into account food rationing".

A message from the Prime Minister warned the people to "stand firm" if invasion came and he went on to say, "The Home Guard, supported by strong mobile columns wherever the enemy's numbers require it, will immediately come to grips with the invaders, and there is little doubt will soon destroy them". Luckily, this optimistic forecast of the Home Guard's capabilities against a ruthless foe was never put to the test. Yet Sir Charles Hallinan, who commanded 3,000 volunteers in the 21st Cardiff Battalion, undoubtedly summed up the spirit of 1940 when he observed, "I'm perfectly certain that if Jerry had come we'd have died with our boots on. We'd have been wiped out, no doubt, but there would have been a fight".

The Home Guard took part in anti-invasion exercises which were held from time to time in the streets of Cardiff. The biggest exercise of the war in South Wales took place on 19-20 October 1941. The *Cardiff Times* reported that, "It brought something like total war to the doorsteps of thousands of homes during Sunday and Monday". The Navy, Army, Air Force, Home Guard and Civil Defence were all involved in a scenario where, under cover of fog, South Wales was being invaded from the Bristol Channel as a diversion to an all-out assault on Southern England. The conclusion drawn from the exercise was that severe damage would have been done to Newport, Cardiff and Barry but the enemy would have suffered heavy casualties, and would have failed to achieve his objectives. The Home Guard succeeded in delaying the invaders sufficiently to give regular troops enough time to counter-attack and drive the enemy back into the sea. The Civil Defence workers also acquitted themselves well in dealing with "devastation" at the power station, post office and railway station. The civilian population continued its normal activities and spectators, especially children, may have regarded such exercises as a form of entertainment. Fortunately, the real thing never happened but imaginary assaults on a city like Cardiff did not appear far fetched at the time.

If the Invader Comes

As the British people contemplated a German assault at any time, emergency measures were put into effect. Church bells were silenced except in the event of an invasion and anything which might help the German army, such as road signs or bus destinations, were removed. Anyone asking for directions came under suspicion and these regulations caused problems for strangers, especially if they were foreigners. In 1940 there were many of these in Cardiff, either in the armed forces or as refugees.

Road blocks and other obstacles were moved into position to obstruct an invading force. Tank traps, such as that at College Road, were still in place as late as 1943. If they were needed, steel shafts could emerge from the plates in the road which, it was hoped, would halt or at least damage an enemy tank. In Ely, where the Home Guard was responsible for manning an anti-tank obstacle, a pill box was built into the wall of the cemetery. Along the St. Fagans road an ingenious makeshift road block was prepared. A heavy pole was mounted at the roadside and attached to it was a mass of barbed wire and an old wagon wheel. When the pole was released the wheel dropped into a deep rut in the road, thus creating a

22.   *Tank trap across Glamorganshire Canal Bridge at College Road 1943.*

formidable obstacle. It was not going to stop a Panzer tank but such defences might hinder an airborne attack and slow down the speed of a German advance. On open spaces, such as Cyncoed Golf Course and the Glider Field at Llanishen, concrete posts, up to 6 feet in height, were driven into the ground to deny enemy gliders a landing ground.

Motorists were urged to drive with extra care in view of the additional hazards now confronting them. Everyone was warned to heed the commands of the Home Guard, "who are an integral part of His Majesty's forces". In some parts of the country, motorists were shot dead for failing to comply with orders to halt. Dr. Emrys Williams of Penylan Road was wounded in the chest at a concealed road block near Bettws-y-Coed in North Wales. He said, "I saw what I thought was a road repair light at the side of the road, when suddenly there was a flash as from a gun and a shattering noise". He had not been challenged but, with invasion scares rife in that summer, such accidents were virtually inevitable.

More than once the church bells rang out to give a false alarm. This happened on one occasion at Cyncoed where 2 members of the Home Guard, equipped with just a single truncheon, answered the call to battle. During that summer, I was a youngster living at Llanmaes Farm in St. Fagans with my mother and my brother. One night she heard a tramping in the yard which sounded like a squad of stormtroopers. Fearfully she peeped out, only to give a sigh of relief when she discovered that 2 or 3 cart horses had escaped from their stable.

Unlikely though it was that an invasion would begin in the Severn Estuary, a decision was made to fortify the island of Flatholm. Initially 2 batteries were installed as a coastal defence but, as the threat of a sea attack disappeared, they were replaced with an anti-aircraft battery. Both Flatholm and Steepholm offered ideal markers for enemy bombers aiming at Cardiff Docks. The garrison at one stage numbered 350 men and the concrete bases of their Nissan huts are still visible. The enemy did eventually set foot on the island when it was declared "non-operational" in 1944 and German prisoners-of-war were given the task of dismantling the installations.

There was a widespread belief that Hitler's success on the continent had been aided by a network of spies feeding rumours and disinformation to a confused population. In Britain, free speech became another rationed item as scare-mongering and defeatist talk were listed as criminal offences. The *Western Mail* hammered the message home by reporting how a man was fined £20 for spreading the alarming news that 20 German parachutists had landed in Kent.

Another campaign reminded people that "Careless talk costs lives". They were told that any scrap of knowledge, however trivial, relating to troop movements, shipping destinations or security at the docks or factories, might be useful to an enemy spy. The Press, while apparently remaining free, was also subject to strict censorship. "A South Wales coast town underwent an intensive fire blitz last night", was how the *Western Mail* reported the air attack on Cardiff in January 1941 and specific details of the raid were not released until some time later.

With supplies of newsprint only 20% of pre-war levels, newspapers were restricted to a maximum of 4-6 pages. Despite censorship and a shortage of paper, the *Echo* always found room for a J.C. Walker cartoon. Often his work had a moving poignancy. On the eve of war, he reflects on the manner in which peace,

SOUTH WALES ECHO AND EXPRESS,   FRIDAY, SEPTEMBER 1, 1939

CARTOON - - - - - - - - - - - - - - - - - - By J. C. WALKER

THE EVACUATION BEGINS

23.   J. C. Walker mourns the departure of peace.

reason and hope are forced to flee in the same way as the children now being uprooted from their homes. Sometimes his humour was satirical, reducing Hitler and Mussolini to figures of fun. On other occasions he tried to bring a smile to people's faces even amid the tragedy of war. His cartoon, showing the reaction of a bemused American after a bomb fell on the Arms Park, is a typical example.

At 6 a.m. on 4 September 1939, police officers raided the houses of all Germans in Cardiff listed as "dangerous" and arrested them. Since the more sinister Nazis such as Kuhnemann had already fled, the majority of these aliens were completely harmless and were soon released. In the summer of 1940, as the fear of imminent invasion intensified, the British adopted a tougher attitude towards potential spies.

All Germans and Austrians in the city were interned as the Government declared Cardiff to be a "protected area". Many of them had come to Wales to escape from the Nazis but no exceptions were allowed. Even German Jewish nurses at the Royal Infirmary were taken away for internment. They were first of all documented at the Law Courts and then handed over to the military authorities at Maindy Barracks. In the prevailing climate, innocent refugees were philosophical about their treatment. Detective Inspector Tom Holdsworth, who worked in the Aliens' Department of the Cardiff Police, arrested an ex-Berliner in Cyncoed, whose wife sobbed amid her tears, "Just like the Gestapo, but Oh! So

24. *Reflections on the destruction of the North Stand in January 1941.*

kind". Spaniards, who had come to this country during the Civil War and were suspected of Fascist sympathies, were also arrested at this time.

There was a strong Italian community in South Wales and in June it was their turn to come under suspicion when Mussolini declared war on Britain. The windows of 2 shops were smashed in Butetown and another dawn raid rounded up Cardiff's Italians, many of whom had lived in the city for more than 20 years. Dabbling in luxury goods on the black market was probably the worst crime any of them had committed and some even had sons in the British forces. Two Italians from Cardiff were among the internees who died aboard the ill-fated *Andorra Star*, when it was torpedoed on its way to Canada.

During that nervous summer, the police were called upon to investigate several spy scares and false alarms. A resident in Ethel Street was reported by a neighbour for tapping messages in Morse code. When he was visited by the police, the culprit turned out to be a leaking water cistern. More serious were reports of parachute landings in Leckwith Woods, which were in fact parachute mines dropped in the Bristol Channel. Two ships were blown up, one at the mouth of the River Ely and another off Penarth Head, before minesweepers were delegated to sweep the channel each morning as a precaution.

Before Dunkirk, there had been a certain amount of tolerance towards those who held pacifist views. The Peace Pledge stall in Cardiff Market launched a petition calling for immediate peace talks. Conscientious objectors were advised how to register their claim and present their appeal at the tribunal. Another refuge for pacifists and conscientious objectors in Penarth was run by 2 former

25. The Great Aluminium Collection.

BBC officials. Less than 2% of men in Wales refused to register for National Service but that was a high enough number to arouse the indignation of a people fighting for their lives. The Peace Pledge stall was closed and the Cardiff City Council dismissed conscientious objectors from its employment. Alderman Williams summed up the prevailing mood, "Every man should have his opinion, but let him pay the price of his opinion". When Councillor J.H. Morgan drew attention to Communist Party meetings in Llandaff Fields, "wilfully helping the spread of unpatriotic propaganda," a decision to outlaw such gatherings was overwhelmingly carried.

In a desperate situation people felt the need to make a patriotic gesture. One measure which boosted morale was Lord Beaverbrook's "pots and pans" appeal. Aluminium, it was claimed, could be used to manufacture aircraft. This was complete nonsense but the appeal was an outstanding success as people dutifully surrendered their saucepans, difficult though they were to replace, as a contribution to the war effort. Items of glass, copper, bronze and aluminium were brought to the WVS collecting point in St. Mary Street. The quantity "exceeded all expectations" and, among the items handed in, was a set of saucepans bought in Germany 15 years earlier. The housewife said she was glad to send them back to their manufacturer in the form of an aeroplane. Collections of aluminium toys were made in schools and one little four-year old swept into the depot in his toy motor car which he had been persuaded to sacrifice for the common good. Altogether, more than a ton of metal was collected.

Later in the war, other sources of scrap metal were to provide useful raw material for the manufacturing of munitions. Fancy wrought iron railings and gates from parks and public buildings were dispatched to the dump at East Moors

26. Jumble sale for the Spitfire Fund at Castleton 1940.

steelworks. A tank from the first World War, which had been on display at Victoria Park, was among the items requisitioned for smelting into new weapons. Where the trams were scheduled to be replaced by trolley buses, the tram lines were dug up to provide 900 tons of scrap. In November 1942 it was the turn of private households to give up their gates and railings. To soften the blow, the *Echo* reported that a privet hedge would look just as attractive and it was worth remembering that one set of household railings could provide up to 100 rifle barrels.

The citizens of Cardiff not only parted with their saucepans in 1940 but also gave their money freely to pay for the production of Spitfires. In August, the Lord Mayor opened a fund to purchase these magnificent aircraft, each of which cost a mere £6,000. Eventually £20,000 was raised with contributions coming from all over the city. Collections were made in the clubs, the pubs and at places of work. A dance, arranged by the Tongwynlais wardens, raised £50 and another substantial sum was raised when villagers at Castleton organised a sale of their fruit and vegetables. Two Cardiff lads spent their August holidays collecting golf balls which they sold to raise 10/- for the fund, while other children sent in their pocket money. Such was the spirit of 1940.

In contrast to previous holidays that year, August Bank Holiday was cancelled and the beaches of Barry Island were virtually deserted. South Wales, in common with the rest of Britain, was working flat out to replace the weapons lost at Dunkirk. The *Western Mail* reflected, "Viewed from a purely parochial standpoint, the weekend was a tragedy, but the greater heartache will be Hitler's, for it proved just how solid the people are in doing their job".

Chapter Three

A People's War

Everyone Will Do His Duty

When invasion was expected any day in September 1940, Winston Churchill declared, "Every man and woman will prepare himself to do his duty, whatever it may be, with special pride and care". After the fall of France, the workers in the factory or the women cultivating the land became as much a part of Britain's war machine as the troops at the front.

Ironically, just as the First World War had contributed to the Great Depression with mass unemployment in areas such as South Wales, so re-armament brought that human tragedy to an end. With the threat from Nazi Germany looming ever larger in the 1930s, a reluctant British government faced up to the necessity of building new armaments factories in those regions which at that time seemed to be out of range from enemy bombers. Cardiff was such an area and, even before the outbreak of hostilities, the city was moving towards a wartime economy. Unemployment in Cardiff had reached a figure of 25% at the height of the Depression. From 1938 onwards it fell so rapidly that by 1944 only 0.2% of those eligible for work were still seeking a job.

The steelworks at East Moors received a major investment of £3 million in 1935 to produce a large integrated steel plant, capable of manufacturing half a million ton of steel a year. By the late 1930s the plant was working to its full capacity, providing the raw material for munitions and ordnance factories in South Wales.

The Edward Curran cartridge case factory in Hurman Street had equipped the guns on the Western Front in the First World War. A new factory was opened on the same site in June 1937 and, by February 1940 when the King and Queen visited the site, it was working 3 shifts around the clock. Before the end of the war, the firm was employing 13,000 workers at factories in or near Cardiff. Production covered a wide range of activities. Millions of cases for cartridges, bombs and shells were manufactured, and more than a million tracks for tanks were produced. Some of the flailing devices, which saved so many lives on D-Day by destroying mines on the beaches, were also built at Currans. The firm also carried out important maintenance work on tanks and aircraft. It was not unusual to see Blenheim bombers, damaged by enemy action, being towed through the

27.   *Women working for victory at Currans.*

streets of Cardiff on their way to Currans for repairs. The company even found the resources to make 26 million much needed domestic utensils for the homes of this country.

A number of sites in South Wales were selected as Royal Ordnance factories when the nation began to rearm. At Cardiff, a site of 47 acres was chosen in Caerphilly Road and work commenced on levelling the site in 1939. Manufacturing began late the following year, even before the roof had been completed. Anti-aircraft guns, pontoon couplings and aircraft cannon were all produced at ROF Llanishen but priority was given to tank and anti-tank guns. In one month during 1944, just before the Allied breakout into Holland, 1,784 tank guns were manufactured, a record for any factory in the British Empire. The majority of the workforce employed in munitions factories were women and among them was Eileen Quick, later Mrs. Watts, who volunteered for work at the ROF in 1941. She recalls cycling across the city, often in the blackout, before commencing a 10 hour shift of hard work amid deafening noise.

Women were to play a vital role in Britain's war effort. Whatever occupation they followed, they responded magnificently to the challenge of total war. Some of them served in the police force or drove ambulances in the blitz. Others worked in the factories or as porters at the docks and the General Station. Industry would have ground to a halt without female labour but, though they often worked 12 hour shifts doing the same tasks as their male colleagues, women were never given the same rate of pay as men.

In the armed forces they carried out many of the tasks which released men for front line duty. They displayed their talents in plotting enemy aircraft movements, maintaining barrage balloons, manning searchlights or anti-aircraft guns, and as radio operators. Many of the WAAFs were trained at St. Athan.

28   *Field gun production at ROF Llanishen.*

Husbands and fathers were suspicious of service life for women, and soldiers often said they would never let their wives enlist in the forces. Yet for sheer courage, nothing matches the heroism of those women who helped the Resistance forces in occupied Europe, often paying for their bravery with their lives.

29.   *Female porters at Cardiff Docks.*

At first the voluntary principle was used to encourage women to enrol for war work. However, as insufficient numbers came forward, female conscription was introduced in March 1941, the first time such a practice had been decreed anywhere in the world. Initially, single girls under 21 were ordered to register for some form of war service but later the age limit was raised to 40. For mothers with young children, there was no compulsion to take up employment but, for those who chose to work, child care was available. It should be remembered that the burden of running the home and looking after the family in wartime fell almost entirely upon women. Even so there were still many mothers who, in addition to caring for their children, took a job or gave a helping hand in the voluntary services.

The Land Army provided a vital new labour force in the battle to feed the nation. Of all the jobs carried out by women during the war, this was one of the most important as Britain was virtually a besieged island until the U-boat menace was defeated. Reta Gale volunteered for the Land Army in 1943 and was stationed at Bryn Golau farm in Llanedeyrn. It was a mixed farm with pigs, sheep and cows. The 70 pigs were fed on waste food collected from cafes, hotels and households, which could then be boiled into a swill. Within a short time Reta became the senior employee on the farm and had learnt a wide range of skills. Farms in Monmouthshire and the Vale of Glamorgan relied on girls like Reta to carry out tasks ranging from haymaking, lambing, driving tractors, hauling logs or picking several hundredweight of potatoes a day. For these back breaking tasks they worked 50 hours a week for a wage of 28/-.

The Land Army was needed for every kind of agricultural work and Phyllis Latham, later to become Mrs. Condon, was employed by the Forestry

30.   Phyllis Condon, second from the right, at Tair Onen Forestry Commission 1943.

Commission between 1941 and 1950. At Tair-Onen, between Bonvilston and Cowbridge, she carried out every process of forestry work from sowing seeds to the felling and trimming of large trees. For many women, war work offered a liberating experience and Phyllis enjoyed the outdoor life on the land and the companionship of her colleagues. They were billeted at St. Fagans, first of all in the Rectory and later in St. Fagans Castle.

Workers were subjected to a discipline which was unthinkable in peacetime. Men and women were directed into specific occupations and absenteeism or lateness for work became a criminal offence. In January 1942 a man, who refused an order to start work as a haulier at Llanbradach Colliery, was given 2 months hard labour, and in April a worker from Tongwynlais was fined £15 for persistently being late for work. His excuse, that "7.45 a.m. was a bit early for him to catch a bus", was not accepted. That was hardly surprising when we remember that over 3,000 workers at Currans factories in Cardiff came from the valleys every day, travelling on special trains and buses. Even with these transport facilities, men and women living in Rhymney or Aberdare had to get up at 4 a.m. to begin the 6 o'clock shift at the factory.

For more than a century the South Wales coalfield had played a vital role in supplying the fuel for British industry. Cardiff had become a great city by exporting Welsh coal to every corner of the globe. After the fall of France the export of coal virtually ceased, as every ton that could be mined was needed for British homes and factories. Old Welsh collieries, which had been closed during the Depression, were re-opened and former miners, often unemployed in the hungry thirties, were urged to return to the industry.

Many were unwilling to do so. At the beginning of the war, wages were poor compared with other industries though there was an improvement later. In addition there were bitter memories and resentment against the coal owners who were held responsible for causing so much misery in the past. Many miners preferred to serve in the armed forces and so the shortage of manpower in the pits became ever more acute. In July 1941 Ernest Bevin appealed for 50,000 ex-miners to return to the pits but more drastic measures were needed to meet the crisis in the coal industry. Initially, the Government took the mines under its own control though it stopped short of full nationalisation. Then in December 1943 Bevin announced that men would be conscripted to work in the mines. They had no choice in the matter and some of the conscripts showed stubborn resistance, refusing to work underground even when threatened with imprisonment. In 1944 there were several such cases. One young man worked only 3 shifts out of 147 while another missed 55 out of 58. Both of them indicated a willingness to serve in the armed forces but were told there could be no exceptions and a month's hard labour was their fate.

Alan Jennings, living at that time in Cathays, was eager to join the RAF as his eighteenth birthday drew nearer. It came as a shock in November 1944 when he discovered that he had been selected by ballot to report for training as a Bevin Boy. His ignorance of mining was complete and four weeks training did little to prepare him for the physical hardship of working at Albion Colliery, Cilfynydd. The coal face was just 3½ feet high and several miles from the pit shaft. Alan's task was to shovel the coal, hacked out by a seasoned collier, on to a conveyor belt.

31. The Bevin Boys.

"The dust, blackness and noise were terrible and the labour relentless". Danger was a constant companion and on one occasion Alan's foot was trapped in a moving conveyor. After two years he was released on medical grounds and still finds confined spaces very claustrophobic. He subsequently joined the RAF and says, "Even the strict discipline of square bashing in the fresh country air of Wiltshire was a pleasurable experience compared with the Albion Colliery".

To compensate for restrictions on personal liberty, Ernest Bevin insisted on better conditions for people at work. Every Currans factory had its own first aid and rest room, together with a fully equipped central clinic for carrying out diagnosis and treatment. Hospital facilities were provided for sick employees and a benevolent fund was created for those in financial distress. Safety first measures at work were supervised by an Accident Prevention Officer and a Factory Committee. An information bureau gave advice on personal problems, such as finding lodgings or obtaining supplementary coupons for working clothes. Gifts of cigarettes and money were sent to the 700 Currans employees in the armed forces. Nowadays these practices would be considered the hallmark of a good employer but they were far from common at that time.

The Port and the Merchant Seamen

Since the heyday of Welsh coal, the ports of Cardiff, Penarth and Barry had declined. Their volume of trade was only 45% of the turnover before the Great

32.   Loading tanks at Cardiff Docks.

War and the dock at Penarth was forced to close in 1936. Three years later it re-opened when the docks of South Wales assumed a new importance with the outbreak of hostilities. The Government took the optimistic view that the Welsh ports, unlike those on the east coast, would be outside the range of the Luftwaffe. In addition, together with Bristol and Liverpool, they were ideally situated to handle vital imports of food, weapons and raw materials from North America.

The docks at Cardiff were run by an emergency committee drawn from the Ministries of Food, Supply and War Transport, together with the dock authorities and the armed services. Later in the war the American forces were represented on the committee. The port soon took on an air of urgency not seen for years. Despite measures taken before the war to modernise the docks, merchant ships arriving at Cardiff and Barry had to wait days and even weeks for a berth in the winter of 1940-41. A third of the nation's vital imports and exports were channelled through the South Wales ports and, if this congestion had continued, Britain might well have lost the war. To meet the crisis, miles of additional railway sidings were laid down, new transit sheds were built and fresh cranes were installed. Rail links to Severn Tunnel Junction were improved and trains flowed through the tunnel every day, including Sundays, which before the war had been a day for maintenance work on the track and tunnel. By the end of hostilities, 25,000 ships had passed through Cardiff Docks and 25 million tons of cargo had been handled. Another 9,000 vessels sailed in and out of Penarth.

None of these measures would have been effective without the cooperation of the dockers themselves. Conciliation committees were set up to deal with labour disputes and, though they were accused of pilfering and dealing in the

33. *To give protection in Mid-Atlantic, this Hurricane is being loaded on to the catapult of a ship in the Queen Alexandra Dock.*

black market, the dockers played their part in ensuring that the port of Cardiff ran as smoothly as possible throughout the war.

In 1941 vital cargoes began to arrive from the United States as part of President Roosevelt's lend lease policy to aid Britain. An American captain was certainly impressed in January of that year when his ship pulled into Cardiff on a Sunday afternoon. A gang of dockers unloaded the goods on deck with such speed that the captain asked whether his cargo was receiving special priority. He was assured that the workmen were following their normal procedure and, as a fresh gang began to empty the hold, the captain commented in admiration, "All this on a blessed Sabbath afternoon. Hell! I never saw anything like it".

Many of the merchant vessels arriving at Cardiff were severely damaged after running the gauntlet of German U-boats. Others arrived in a dilapidated state as their heavily laden cargoes shifted in the gales of a North Atlantic crossing. The 8 dry docks at Cardiff, with their long tradition of maritime maintenance, were strained to the limit as ships queued up in the Bristol Channel awaiting repair. In addition to handling repairs, the Channel Dry Docks at Cardiff fitted ships with degaussing apparatus to protect them against magnetic mines.

The most extraordinary repair job of the war was carried out on the *Tafelberg*, a vessel of 21,000 tons, which ended up on the beach at Barry after being mined and broken in half. The 2 sections were temporarily fitted together and then towed to the Channel Dry Dock. The parts were rejoined and the ship was converted into a tanker, renamed the *Empire Heritage*. The vessel, now as good as new, began a fresh career on the dangerous North Atlantic route. Unfortunately its ill luck continued and, on its second voyage, the *Empire Heritage* was torpedoed and sunk.

34.   *The Tafelberg is towed into Cardiff for repair.*

The docks at Cardiff were to provide training facilities for one of the most daring exploits of the war. Captain Bill Pritchard, a Cardiff Territorial Army officer, came up with an idea to destroy the lock gates and dock installations at St. Nazaire, thus denying the port as a base for the mighty German battleship, *Tirpitz*.

35.   *The Merchant Seamen's Memorial in Cardiff Bay.*

For two weeks, commandos trained between the lock gates of the Roath Basin in preparation for the assault. At the same time, in the Bute Dry Dock, they experimented with explosives on a ship which served as a replica for the *Campbelltown*, the vessel chosen for a spectacular ending to its career.

When the raid on St. Nazaire took place in March 1942, the *Campbelltown* was converted into a delayed action bomb and rammed the dock gates at a speed of 20 knots. The commandos swarmed ashore to sabotage key installations and, 12 hours after the start of the operation, the *Campbelltown* exploded, wrecking the biggest dry dock in occupied Europe. St. Nazaire would never accommodate the *Tirpitz* or any other German battleship but the price of success was costly. More than half of the attacking force of 600 men were killed or captured. Captain Pritchard, who was last seen running through the dockyard in the vicinity of the *Campbelltown,* was among the fatalities. Five Victoria crosses were awarded, two of them posthumously, which is an indication of the courage displayed in the raid.

Britain's merchant seamen take their place among the greatest heroes of the Second World War. The fleet of ships sailing from the ports of South Wales amounted to 164 ships. Of these, 123 were sunk by enemy action. The Reardon Smith Company, a famous Cardiff shipping firm, lost 33 of its 41 ships, while Evan Thomas and Radcliffe lost 10 from its fleet of 24. Much more poignant than the material losses were the fatalities among the sailors who struggled to keep Britain's lifeline open against the merciless onslaught of the German U-boats. Appropriately, a memorial in Cardiff Bay pays tribute to the brave seamen of the merchant navy who saved Britain from starvation and defeat.

An article in the *Cardiff Times* on 7 February 1942 gives an indication of their courage. A few days after he had celebrated his 17th birthday, Patrick Meehan from Ethel Street was forced to take to the lifeboats, the second time this had happened to him in his young life. His ship had been torpedoed and he with 20 other Welshmen, mostly from Cardiff, were adrift for 14 days. They killed an albatross to ease their hunger and thirst but, when rescue came, it was too late for one of the Cardiff seamen. He died just as the rescue ship drew alongside, while Patrick himself had badly sunburned legs and a poisoned hand after climbing down the rope ladder into the boat.

James Slater, a second officer with the Morel Company of Cardiff, sailed with a convoy which left Bermuda for Britain in November 1940. Only 10 out of 38 ships completed this voyage. One of the vessels sent to the bottom of the ocean by a German torpedo was the *Glanely*. Before sinking, the ship managed to launch its lifeboats but these were caught in a cross-fire as the U-boat surfaced to attack the vessel coming to their aid. All 42 members of the *Glanely's* crew were lost, among them a 15 year old cabin boy. Slater's own ship, the *Jersey*, survived this voyage but was sunk by a mine in the Suez Canal in 1942.

Preparing for the Blitz

During the war, most men and women carried out voluntary duties in addition to their everyday work. In the 1930s, believing that air raids would result in horrendous casualties, the Government appealed for volunteers to serve as

36.   Air Raid wardens at their headquarters in Insole Court.

special constables, air raid wardens and part-time auxiliary firemen. At first recruits were slow to come forward and Sir John Anderson, visiting Cardiff in February 1939, called for more volunteers to carry out these vital duties. He pointed out that Cardiff was 1,000 men under strength in the Territorial Army, 1,800 men short in the Auxiliary Fire Service and there was still a need for 2,000 special constables. He urged that it was not a question of "rendering a service to the government of the day but . . . a matter of self-help and protection".

As early as 1936, the Home Office had set up an air raid wardens' organisation to recruit volunteers who would be trained to deal with small fires and help the public during an aerial attack. The wardens' headquarters in Cardiff was originally at the Law Courts but in April 1940 it was moved to Insole Court. The success of the voluntary principle is underlined by the fact that the city was authorised to enrol 500 paid wardens but never found it necessary to appoint more than 45. Nearly 4,000 men and women had come forward to serve in the city's 94 wardens' posts or sectors by May 1940.

However, the Chief Warden appealed for another 1,500 men and women and when the air raids began that target was soon reached. Herbert Morrison, the Home Secretary, visited Cardiff in November to inspect Civil Defence forces and was lavish in his praise of their public spirit: "I do not think there is another city in the country that can equal your record – 6,000 wardens and only 30 or so paid". In the early days of the war, the wardens were not popular figures. With their catchphrase, "Put that light out," they were often accused of being "tin pot Hitlers" or "twirps and a nuisance to everyone", doing little but play cards while they were on duty. It was to be a different story in the blitz when they showed their courage and won the respect of the community.

37. NFS parade in Westgate Street 1943.

The nerve centre of the Fire Service was in Westgate Street. A lookout post above the six-storied fire station proved to be an excellent viewpoint for looking across the city to see where the worst conflagrations were taking place. Eighteen other auxiliary fire stations were established by October 1939 and Insole Court was used for training purposes and the storage of equipment. The auxiliary volunteers were given 60 hours training and gained experience in fire fighting by assisting the regular brigade. Women as well as men served in the AFS. At the outbreak of war, William James was based at a fire station using the premises of Romilly Road garage. Later he joined the merchant navy and was killed at sea. It was then that his widow, 18 year old Frankie James, enlisted in the transport division of the fire service at Cathedral Road. Though not actively involved in firefighting, Mrs. James was often in attendance at fires as part of the fuel tanker crew who followed the pumps during raids.

In 1939 the resources of the Fire Service were extremely limited. The suburb of Cathays, for instance, was restricted to 2 fire fighting teams, each with 5 men. They were equipped with a ladder, a stirrup pump, a trailer pump, canvas buckets and a taxi to take them to any emergency which might arise. Fortunately, there was time to train and organise the volunteers before the blitz began in all its fury. Many of the auxiliaries became full-time firemen and in August 1941 a logical step was taken when auxiliaries and regulars merged to form the National Fire Service.

As the danger from air raids increased, every house was given access to a sandbag which could be used to extinguish an incendiary bomb before it gained a hold. In June 1940 another safety measure was implemented when the Chief Constable made an appeal for "stirrup pump brigades" in every street. They were given 1½ hours training by the fire brigade to make them capable of dealing with small fires. When the raids began, more than 500 streets had organised fire watching patrols on a rota basis and often they provided their own equipment.

At the outbreak of war, 22,000 Anderson shelters had been delivered to the city and some householders looked on them as a challenge to their DIY skills. The *South Wales Echo* reported that Thomas Jones of Glynne Street in Canton had given the interior walls of his shelter a coat of cream paint, fitted it with lighting and an electric fire, and finally planted flowers on the top. The reporter complimented him on the way he had combined "utility with beauty", though it is likely that within a year or two vegetables had replaced the flowers. With a thick covering of soil on top, these dugout retreats in the garden did offer real protection unless a house was unlucky enough to receive a direct hit. Public information films, showing people snug and cosy in the bunk beds of their shelter, were designed to persuade families to use them. The Anderson shelter saved numerous lives during the blitz but unfortunately they could be bitterly cold with a tendency to flood after heavy rain. Consequently, many people preferred to take their chances under the stairs.

Personal protection for those without a garden was not provided until February 1941 when the Morrison shelter became available. It was a box like cage which nearly filled the room in many homes and often fulfilled an additional purpose as a dining table. The owners of the Lych Gate cafe in Llandaff found it an excellent means of displaying their cakes.

Plans had been made to evacuate the Cardiff Royal Infirmary in an emergency but war was declared before a more elaborate scheme, to provide a deep underground shelter between Glossop Terrace and the main hospital, could

38.   The Anderson Shelter saved many a life.

be completed. Nevertheless, by the autumn of 1940 air raid wardens were on duty at the hospital and a fire watching rota had been drawn up. Dispatch riders were also standing by to summon surgeons and anaesthetists from their homes in an emergency. The Tredegar ward was equipped as a resuscitation unit with trained operating and anaesthetic teams, all of whom were capable of dealing with cases requiring blood transfusion or preparation for urgent operations.

Finally, the work of the Women's Voluntary Service should not be forgotten. Their motto was, "If it should be done, the WVS will do it". Its members staffed British Restaurants and mobile canteens for the troops. They provided cups of tea for the people who were homeless or were taking cover in a public shelter. They also collected salvage, assisted in the billeting of evacuees, ran nurseries for working mums, and organised every kind of activity from jam making to knitting comforts for the troops.

By the autumn of 1940 the Battle of Britain had been won. Valuable time had been gained since the onset of war to make the essential preparations which would give the people of Cardiff some protection against the Luftwaffe. The training of the civil defence workers and the measures taken to survive the blitz would soon be tested to the full. Hitler, having failed to invade Britain, now set out to destroy the morale of its people by raining terror from the skies.

Chapter Four

The Blitz

The Ordeal Begins

Measures were taken to defend Cardiff before the full fury of the blitz began. Anti-aircraft guns were ringed around the city and rocket guns on Ely Racecourse were strategically placed to deter low flying aircraft. Mobile guns, mounted on lorries, were also deployed. The approach of enemy raiders was plotted at the control room of the Observer Corps in Ely Rise where the Fairwater Conservative Club now stands. One of its tasks was to help our own aircraft if they were in difficulties and the corps took a pride in its reputation as "the eyes and ears of the RAF".

In 1941, however well defences were coordinated, it was difficult to offer very much protection against raids carried out at night. When an attack appeared likely, the "yellow alert" was given by the air raid siren. Employees were expected to carry on working at this stage though it was obviously time to start taking sensible precautions. Alf Colley, working at the goods yard, recalled the time when a train of oil wagons entered the yard during a yellow warning and its driver was greeted by an inspector with a bellow, "Get that ruddy thing out of here in double quick time". When raiders were overhead, everyone switched to "red alert" and, if they were able to do so, withdrew to the shelters. In all, Cardiff was put on red alert 585 times between June 1940 and May 1944.

The port was a prime target and naturally it was strongly defended. Barrage balloons, many of them moored on vessels in the Bristol Channel, hovered overhead and the lock entrances into the harbour were guarded with heavy, steel wire anti-torpedo nets. Anti-aircraft guns were manned by the regular army during the blitz but in 1943 their duties were taken over by the Docks Home Guard. When the alert sounded, men left their work to man the guns until the raid was over. Their duties continued until the summer of 1944 when the guns were removed to the South Coast to meet the onslaught from Hitler's V1s.

Partly as a result of these precautions, the port suffered surprisingly little damage during the blitz. Its history records that 300 bombs fell in the docks area but only 3 ships were damaged and 11 workers killed. The report observed, "The port was lucky, amazingly lucky", though much of the credit goes to its fire brigade and civil defence workers. The greatest disruption was caused when the

39.   *The damaged SS Stesso following the raid of 20 June 1940.*

40.   *The sinking of the San Felipe on 9 July 1940.*

Germans laid mines in the channel. This was a regular occurrence which continued until 1942 and sometimes the port was closed for days until the channel could be swept clear.

The people of Cardiff had good reason to be grateful for its lush, open spaces. When the blitz began, many bombs fell harmlessly on such locations as Bute Park, Cyncoed golf course or the countryside around the city. Flares at Michaelston-le-Pit, Llanedeyrn and Leckwith Moors were used as decoys to attract bombs intended for such vital installations as the East Moors steelworks or the ROF at Llanishen. The ruse was a success as production at the East Moors Works was never seriously affected, while no bombs at all fell on the ordnance factory. Tragically, however, an anti-aircraft shell penetrated its roof in March 1944, killing 9 workers and injuring 33 others.

After the fall of France, Cardiff was well within the range of the Luftwaffe, flying from its newly captured bases in Brittany. The port suffered its first attack in the early hours of 20 June 1940 when a lone raider dropped 16 bombs. Most of them fell harmlessly but the SS *Stesso*, moored in the East Dock, was damaged after being hit in the stern. No lives were lost and the ship was later refloated.

A few weeks later, on a sunny afternoon, a worse tragedy occurred when the *San Fillipe* received a direct hit. The bomb exploded in the hold, killing 6 men. This was the day Tim O'Brien from David Street earned his reputation as the "hero of the docks". The lower rungs of the ladder having been blown away, he jumped into the hold and plunged into the smoking inferno. Three times he risked his life to rescue his injured mates by pulling them into a tub which could

41.   *Angus Street in September 1940.*

then be hauled to the surface. Later, he received an industrial award for his courage. Another hero during this sudden attack was J.N. Anderson, a porter and first aid worker, who made a precarious descent down a rope to help the injured men. His gallant conduct won him the British Empire Medal.

One of the earliest tests for the Cardiff firemen came in August 1940, when a Nazi bomber swept down from the skies over Pembroke Dock and unloaded a stick of bombs on the oil tanks. The fire and smoke from 3 million gallons of blazing oil twisted and turned hundreds of feet in the air. For 3 weeks, 650 firemen grappled with the blazing inferno, continuing the struggle even when they were bombed and machine-gunned in a subsequent attack. Five members of the Cardiff AFS lost their lives when the fuel in one of the tanks erupted and engulfed them in the flames. George medals were awarded to 13 firemen, 3 of them from Cardiff, for their heroic deeds in this grim portent of the testing times to come.

Daylight raids over Cardiff in that summer and autumn of 1940 usually involved no more than one or two aircraft. Even so, a single raider was enough to strike sudden terror into people on the ground, especially if there was no time to sound the alert. In those days the boys at Canton High School used Ely Racecourse as their playing field, and one day in September a rugby match was in progress when the approach of an aeroplane could be heard. Everyone went on playing, assuming the plane to be "one of ours". Suddenly it began to open fire, forcing all the boys and their teacher to dive for cover.

These early probings by the Luftwaffe were usually directed at the docks but on 3 September bombs were dropped in the district of Roath, where a house in Arabella Street was "cut from adjoining premises as if by a giant knife". Angus Street, Moy Road and Claude Place, where an oil bomb set 3 properties ablaze, all suffered damage and loss of life. There were 46 casualties that night, 11 of them fatal.

Twelve days later the Cardiff Royal Infirmary had its baptism by fire when 70 casualties were admitted to the Tredegar Ward after another "hit and run" raid. The same night a major disaster at the hospital was averted when a 500-pound bomb fell on Longcross Street, leaving a crater 8 feet deep. Luckily it failed to explode but six months later the hospital was not to be so fortunate.

Up until this time, South Wales had been visited by enemy aircraft on more occasions than anywhere else in Britain and representatives from the Civil Defence organisations came from London and other cities to see how similar services were coping in Cardiff. The raids at this stage, involving a few bombers at a time, were to continue until the end of 1940, acting as a grim rehearsal for the much greater ordeal to come in the New Year.

A Night of Terror

On 2 January 1941 Cardiff was confronted with the reality of modern warfare. It was a bitterly cold night with traces of an earlier snowfall still on the ground. A full moon penetrated the blackout and when the sirens wailed at

6.37 p.m. the bombardment began. Only about 100 aircraft were involved in the raid but they inflicted grievous wounds upon the city. First of all, flares and incendiary bombs began to light up the landscape below with an eerie green light. Where they fell on the open spaces of Sophia Gardens, Leckwith and the Castle grounds, there was "a grotesque scene as the little fire bombs performed their dance of death". Soon afterwards high explosives and parachute mines followed in the wake of these illuminations. In the hours that followed, the value of months of training undertaken by the emergency services and their volunteers became apparent.

Riverside was the first suburb of Cardiff to feel the full onslaught of the Luftwaffe. The district suffered the heaviest casualties in the city as more than 60 people lost their lives in the first half hour of the raid. Norman Harris, whose father had a grocery shop on the corner of Wyndham Street, has vivid memories of that terrible night. "Minutes after the siren sounded the alert, the area was saturated with incendiary bombs, soon to be followed by high explosives and landmines". An incendiary fell on their shop and became lodged in the flat roof. Norman climbed on to the roof in an unsuccessful attempt to reach it and, as he was clambering down, another bomb fell nearby and blew him through the back door. Dazed as he was, Norman noticed a gas lamp post shorn in half with its gas blazing merrily away. His home and the family shop were destroyed in the ensuing fire but luckily no-one was seriously injured.

Later that night the family had another narrow escape on their way to Leckwith Avenue where they stayed for a time with relatives. As they were walking along Ninian Park Road, they noticed a parachute dangling precariously

42.   *Blackstone Street, devastated after the raid of 2 January 1941.*

43. De Burgh Street after the blitz.

from the roof of a house. Only next day did they learn that it was an unexploded
landmine. These deadly devices were the most destructive weapons of the blitz.
Capable of wreaking devastating havoc on impact, they gently floated down and
were liable to land anywhere according to the vagaries of the wind.

Mourners, who had attended a funeral earlier in the day, were gathered
together at a house in Blackstone Street. When the bombing began, they decided
it was safer to remain indoors rather than make a dash for the public shelter. It was
a decision that cost 7 of them their lives when a landmine struck the house. A
motor car parked outside was blown to pieces and part of it was later found
hanging from a tree in Neville Street, a hundred yards away. Nowadays, the
maisonettes of Edinburgh Court occupy the site where Blackstone Street was
destroyed on that ghastly night.

Not far away in Neville Street, another 7 people were killed in a single house
and in De Burgh Place the Riverside Conservative Club was among the buildings
reduced to rubble. Further along the road, a rescue party dug for 6 hours to bring
out a six year old boy, crouched under the shattered stairs. They were guided to
him as he sang *God save the King*, the only tune he claimed to know.

The most horrifying episode of the raid occurred in Grangetown, where
Hollyman's bakery occupied the junction of Stockland Street and Corporation
Road. The basement at the rear had been reinforced as a shelter and when the
siren sounded people hurried to take cover. Soon after the attack began, a high
explosive bomb hit the bakery and 32 people in the basement, including the
Hollyman family, were killed. Bernard Moorcraft, later a city councillor, lived
across the road from the bakery. He and his family were on their way to the
shelter, "but things outside were so intense we had to go back in. The next time
we went to the front door to try again . . . there was no Hollyman's there".

44.   The destruction of Llandaff Cathedral.

No-one had survived and after the wardens brought out what human remains they could find, the cellar was filled in.

Not far away the gasworks in Grangetown was lit up by the flames. Two landmines missed the target but one gas holder erupted in a burst of fire as a third explosion scored a direct hit. Two others were damaged and gas mains throughout the city were affected for nearly a week before the supply was fully restored. Ironically the *South Wales Echo* had carried a story earlier that day, stating that, "bombs cannot blow up British gas holders".

Just before 8 o'clock, Clifford Smith, on duty with the Home Guard at Llandaff Institute, noticed a parachute drifting lazily towards the cathedral. At first he thought it was an airman baling out but, as he made his way downstairs, he heard a thunderous roar. Probably the cords of the parachute became entangled in the spire of the cathedral before a landmine exploded outside the south porch. Incredibly the porch was only slightly damaged but the summit of the spire was dislodged. A huge crater erupted among the ancient graves in the churchyard and tombstones were hurled like ancient missiles more than half a mile away. A few weeks later, when censorship of the raid was lifted, *The Times* reported that, "The whole of the nave and the south side were unroofed from end to end . . . stout oaken doors were split like matchwood and torn from their hinges. The interior of the cathedral was a scene of desolation. The floor was cluttered with fallen timber and broken slates, heavy pews had been thrown about and broken, and the organ severely damaged". The beautiful great west window and the stone tracery on the southern side were in tatters. Other windows too were reduced to fragments but fortunately 12 priceless stained glass windows had been removed to a place of safety a few months earlier. The famous Rossetti Tryptych, *The Seed of*

45.　*The shattered nave of the Cathedral.*

David, was also spared thanks to the foresight of placing it in a packing case behind some sandbags.

The dean and head verger were discussing fire precautions inside the cathedral when the raid began. The dean could not find his steel helmet and settled for a colander to protect his head. He suffered injuries but not as badly as Bob White, the verger, who was thrown under the debris near the lectern and lost his speech for a time afterwards. Only Coventry, among British cathedrals, suffered greater damage than Llandaff.

The clergy continued to hold services, first of all at the Llandaff Institute and soon afterwards at the Prebendal House. The top of the cathedral spire was dismantled because it was a hazard but a temporary asbestos screen was built in the Presbytery arch. This allowed the Lady Chapel and the Sanctuary, the only areas still intact, to be used for worship. In April 1942 a service of reconciliation was held to celebrate the re-opening of this part of the cathedral. The nave remained open to the skies for many years and, together with the truncated spire, it remained a symbol of martyrdom at this ancient place of worship.

Though many people wept when they looked upon their beloved cathedral the morning after the blitz, there was also a sense of relief that, despite the devastation, no-one was killed. If the mine had landed 50 yards away, most of the village and its inhabitants would have been blown to pieces. As it was Llandaff presented a sorry sight the next day. Windows were shattered and slates were missing from the roofs of every building in High Street as a result of the blast. At St. Michael's College, four houses were destroyed and the students' quarters were wrecked. Luckily the students were still on vacation and no-one was hurt, but the chapel was ruined and many of the college records destroyed.

Inaccurate bombing at night was always as likely to hit a civilian target as a military one. Considerable damage was caused to the Isolation Hospital near Lansdowne Road and at Llandough Hospital, where the Matron's quarters and nursing accommodation were wrecked and for a time only 3 out of 10 wards were habitable. In both cases, as luck would have it, there were no casualties and everywhere the work of the hospitals continued throughout the raid.

That January night is etched forever in the memory of those who experienced it. At the City Lodge, now St. David's Hospital, Betty Dancey was giving birth to her baby daughter when bombs began to fall on Riverside. Following a huge explosion, Betty was hastily wrapped in blankets and taken to the shelter. She was given a sedative, including a brandy, and when she came round she heard a voice saying, "I can't tell you where to put them, the mortuary's full". Fearing the worst, Betty was reassured when a nurse told her she was lying under a bed as all the windows in the ward had been shattered.

"The management advises patrons to leave", was the warning message flashed on the screen of the cinemas when an air raid began. Sometimes people left the theatre but the majority usually stayed to watch the film. On 2 January a crowded audience in the Canton cinema was watching *Night Train to Munich*. Three incendiary bombs fell through the roof and landed in the aisle alongside the 9d seats. The packed auditorium burst into flames but there was no panic as people quietly moved away, allowing members of the staff to deal with the fire. As it had not been used for years and was full of moth holes, only a dribble of water came

46.   *Glamorgan Street after the blitz.*

out of the fire hose. Eventually the fire was extinguished with buckets of sand and customers returned to their seats to enjoy the rest of the show.

Unfortunately, their nonchalance did not receive its just reward as the police ordered the evacuation of the cinema soon afterwards. Canton High School had been hit by an oil bomb which led to the destruction of the Boys' Department on the upper floor. The school gates were locked and there was a delay before the firemen could tackle the blaze. The fire was soon out of control and acted like a beacon for the enemy bombers overhead. As a consolation, the intrepid patrons of the Canton cinema were given a ticket to come and see the rest of the film the following night.

Eileen Quick was enjoying the pantomime at the New Theatre when the raid began. The show continued for a while amid deafening noise until the manager brought proceedings to a halt. He suggested that everyone should remain in the theatre as it was extremely dangerous to venture outside. The audience entertained themselves with a singsong and children were encouraged to come on the stage and take part in an impromptu performance. At last the siren sounded the "all clear" and Eileen, with her mother, sister and cousin, began to hurry home.

As they crossed Cardiff Bridge they could see Canton and Riverside lit up like day and near the City Lodge a plate glass window blew out, missing them by inches. Thomas and Evans, the grocer's shop on the corner of Kings Road, was burning fiercely and the stench of burning fat amid its charred rubble was to remain for weeks afterwards. Thankfully the Quicks arrived home in Glamorgan Street and went to bed just as the wailing of the siren announced that the raiders had returned. The family barely had time to take cover under the kitchen table when there was a tremendous bang. A dresser full of beautiful crockery, Mrs.

47.   Croft Street and Rose Street in January 1941.

Quick's pride and joy, came crashing down and as Mr. Quick went to open his front door he found it was no longer there. Across the road was a huge, gaping hole where a bomb had struck Gould's bakery and killed Mrs. Gould and 7 other people.

The little streets near City Road in Roath endured as great an ordeal as anyone on this terrifying night. Properties on the corner of Croft Street and Rose Street, where 9 people lost their lives, were completely destroyed. In nearby Talworth Street, the same stick of bombs claimed 4 more victims. Casualties were also heavy in the Docks area. Bute Street suffered severe damage and nearly 20 people were killed, among them 3 Norwegian seamen. One of the most hair-raising incidents of the night occurred near Caerphilly Road, when an unexploded mine fell on some allotments. Half a dozen householders tried to pull it away from its crater, thinking it was a fragment of an enemy bomber, and did not realise they could be blown to pieces at any moment.

In the city centre, a landmine created a huge crater on the Cardiff Arms Park, 15 metres in diameter and 4 metres in depth. The grandstand and terraces at the river end were seriously damaged but a much worse human disaster would have occurred if the mine had drifted a little further towards the Westgate Street flats. Ironically, a few months earlier a _Western Mail_ reader had suggested using the steel from the stand as scrap metal, since it was neither aesthetically pleasing nor likely to be needed for the foreseeable future.

Amid the moonlight and the flames, Cardiff's Civic Centre, its white Portland stone giving it the appearance of a gigantic wedding cake about to be devoured, seemed to be presenting itself as a sacrifice. Miraculously, it was spared as hundreds of incendiaries descended in a cascade, 30 of them landing on the roof of the City Hall alone. Firewatchers and firemen quickly raked them into the street below where they were smothered or extinguished in the Glamorganshire Canal.

These bombs had caused serious fires all over the city and the fire service received more than 170 calls during the night. Even with the assistance of reinforcements from other brigades, resources were soon stretched to the limit. The firemen were further hampered by the freezing temperatures which had put water pipes and hoses out of action. Happily, following the destruction created by incendiaries in the raid on London a few days earlier, firewatching was now compulsory. Despite the enormity of the firemen's task, every blaze was subdued, often with the assistance of the public. Wardens, the Home Guard, servicemen on leave and other members of the public did what they could to smother the deadly fireballs. Where possible, this was done with sand which was available from public shelters or street corners. Unfortunately, on this bitterly cold night, the sand was sometimes frozen and many a brave soul removed his coat to extinguish the flames before they became dangerous.

Civil defence workers and rescue squads endured the hail of death from the skies in their determination to reach and aid people who were trapped or wounded among the carnage. Doctors, often lying on their stomachs amid the debris, gave morphia to the wounded. To reach injured victims, men and women drove their ambulances through streets strewn with craters, lit only by the flames of burning buildings. Falling masonry was just one of the hazards the rescue

48. Restoring essential services in Newport Road.

workers faced as they fought their way through the wreckage of collapsing buildings. Often the inhabitants were past helping but sometimes faint cries from those buried under the rubble inspired them to redouble their efforts.

Gathering and dispensing information was vital. Messengers, many of them young lads, braved the bombing to run errands while female telephonists worked for 26 hours without a break to keep communications open. Three St. John's Ambulance cadets were awarded the order's Certificate of Merit for their work as messengers in the Cardiff West control area. Communications throughout the district had been crippled but Leonard Weekes, Robert Wilcox and Windsor Rogers continued to gather and pass on information. In addition, despite instructions not to risk their lives, they also fought fires, cleared rubble and helped victims suffering from shock.

The "all clear" sounded at 4.50 a.m. but few people went to bed. As dawn broke, fires were still smouldering and the aftermath of destruction could be seen in every part of the city. Gas, electricity and water mains were in urgent need of repair and dangerous craters in the road were a further hazard. Householders were advised to boil all supplies of water and milk in case they were contaminated. In Glamorgan Street, the Quick family were rationed to 2 buckets of water a day for washing, cooking and sanitation, a state of affairs that lasted for two weeks.

There were many people who had an unpleasant surprise when they returned home after the raid. Dick Ryan was at a party in Cathays and waited there until the bombing ceased. He walked home and, as he opened the front door of his house in Wyndham Crescent, it collapsed. Going inside he looked up to find that, in place of the roof, there was now a starry sky. Howard Harris had an even traumatic experience when he returned to his home in Wyndham Street. He was a telegraph boy and was not released from duty until after the raid. He must have feared the worst when he found the house wrecked and did not know what had happened to his family. They were safe but found it impossible to leave a message for him.

On 2 January Edward Bush, who was 8 years old at the time, had just come home to Jubilee Street in Grangetown after visiting relatives in Port Talbot. His parents took him to the Olympia cinema to see *"It's in the Air"*, a film starring George Formby. When the warning notice came on the screen, his father decided

49.   *Jubilee Street as Edward Bush found it.*

to drive back to Port Talbot. As they passed Kingsway, they saw a group of soldiers extinguishing incendiary bombs by stamping on them with their boots. Edward recalls seeing Cardiff "lit up like a fairground" as he looked down on the blazing city from the top of The Tumble. Next day, when the Bush family returned home, they found their house completely destroyed and their neighbours across the road among the fatalities of the raid. By a strange quirk, among the ruins Edward found his Hornby train set, the only item in the house that was undamaged.

As a result of the raid, 95 homes were totally destroyed, 233 so badly damaged that demolition was the only alternative, and another 426 houses were uninhabitable until repairs were made. In the depths of winter, the homeless, dazed and shaken by their ordeal, needed immediate assistance. Wardens, civil defence workers and police shepherded them to rest centres, where they were comforted, given temporary shelter and offered a meal, before they began the search for new accommodation.

Several householders were temporarily evacuated from houses where unexploded bombs had caused considerable disruption. There were nearly 50 of these bombs scattered around the city and 8 of them were landmines. Occupants of a house in danger were always evacuated to safety and the wisdom of this precaution was shown when a landmine fell on Prospect Drive in Llandaff but did not explode until the following day. Any occupants would almost certainly have been killed. Dealing with unexploded bombs was the most nerve racking task anyone had to undertake in the blitz. These fiendish weapons were dropped with delayed action detonators intended to cause maximum disruption. They were armed with a variety of devices which might erupt at any time and were completely unpredictable. Inevitably, the mortality rate from these death traps was

50.   Bud Fisher with his "Bomb Disposal" truck.

very high and the bomb disposal section of the Royal Engineers was satirically dubbed the "Suicide Squad". Not all the men who risked their lives in this most dangerous of jobs were regular soldiers for among them were members of the Home Guard and civilian workers.

One volunteer was Bud Fisher, service manager of Merrett and Stephen, who refused to part with his new five-ton truck when the army tried to commandeer it. Instead he drove it himself, risking his life by loading landmines on to the vehicle before taking them to a quarry where they could be rendered harmless. Years later he reflected on his first call to a mine in the castle grounds. He was told to remove everything metallic in case the mine was magnetic. He pointed out that the truck itself was made of metal so he was told to drive around the bomb, keeping 200 feet away. "It felt as though someone was pouring ice cold water down my back". His narrowest escape came at Llandough when there was a shout that the mine was ticking. Everyone fled to safety and no-one was hurt but,

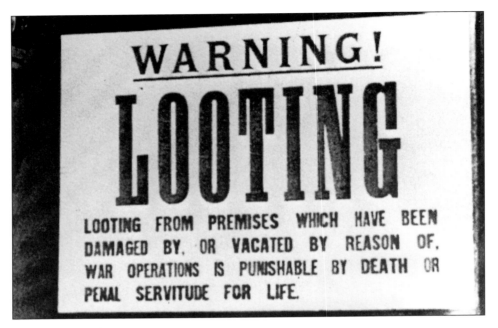

51.   *Warning to looters.*

as the mine exploded with a great roar, one man was left standing naked apart from his shoes.

The police and wardens remained on patrol in the evacuated areas, partly to ensure that no-one was putting himself in danger, but also to apprehend looters. This was one of the darker aspects of the blitz. Despite the threat of severe punishment, these parasites robbed premises which could no longer be secured. It was not unknown for thieves to break open gas meters to steal the coins. Even more despicable was the practice of looting a wrecked building where the inhabitants might be lying dead or wounded among the rubble. No-one left a damaged dwelling for long unless they had first boarded up all possible entrances. Though notices proclaimed that "looting is punishable by death or penal servitude for life", such drastic penalties were never imposed. However, anyone guilty of this despicable crime was certain to face imprisonment. In March 1941 Patrick O'Brien was sentenced to 3 terms of penal servitude after being found guilty on 3 charges of looting and stealing from bombed houses. The police found him carrying away a number of carpets and, when his house was searched, other stolen articles were found. Considerable resentment was also felt toward motorists who toured blitzed areas after the raid, often impeding those still trying to clear the wreckage.

A few months earlier a suggestion was made by the Watch Committee to impose a curfew. It was argued that there were too many people in the city centre at night, while motor cars might hamper the emergency services during an air raid. The Commissioner for Civil Defence decided that a curfew would undermine morale and the only restrictive measure to be imposed was a decision to close theatres by 10 p.m. Events proved that the Commissioner's faith in the

52. *Mass funeral at Cathays Cemetery in January 1941.*

people was justified and the citizens of Cardiff earned plaudits for the calm manner in which they faced their first big test. When the raid began, some people in the city centre risked the falling bombs to reach their homes, while others took to the safety of the shelters at the castle.

Just a few hours before the raid began the *South Wales Echo* headline read: "RAF havoc on German factories - paid back in their own coin". The Germans subsequently claimed that the bombing of Cardiff was their response to that attack on Bremen. Whatever the motive, more than 150 people died a violent death in Cardiff on 2-3 January 1941 and the eventual toll rose to 165. Six days later many of the victims were buried in a civic funeral at Cathays cemetery. Not all of them could be identified and some shared a common grave. The procession of mourners included the Lord Mayor, wearing black crepe on his chain of office, and members of the Corporation. The Bishop of Llandaff led the funeral service and, in its reporting of the ceremony, the *South Wales Echo* commented, "High and low, young and old, mingled around the communal graves while they tearfully but silently honoured the dead. It was a scene that those who witnessed it will forever have indelibly printed on their minds".

The Later Raids

While the Luftwaffe never again struck with the same ferocity, attacks upon Cardiff were to continue for the next two years. On 26 February the raiders returned and 4 people were killed in Violet Place near Whitchurch Common. On the same night, St. Martin's Church in Albany Road was destroyed by incendiary bombs. The vicar, Canon Brown, was cycling home when he heard that his church was on fire. He rushed there to assist the fire brigade but the flames were already devouring the whole building. "The next morning I went out and it was just a smoking shell".

The following week, on 3 March, Cardiff was attacked in what was described as, "one of the greatest fire raids of the war". Considering the severity of the attack, casualties were relatively light compared with earlier raids but extensive damage was inflicted on property, especially in the Roath district. The Chief Constable commented, "I doubt if any town has had more incendiary bombs showered upon it in one raid. It was a real pyrotechnic display".

A torrent of these incendiaries descended on Roath Road Church at the junction of City Road and Newport Road. Fire watchers raised the alarm, hoping to save one of the finest Wesleyan chapels in Wales, but the blaze was so intense that the building was soon reduced to ashes. The gaunt skeleton of the building remained a familiar landmark until 1955, when the Methodist Council decided to sell the site which eventually became the social security offices at Heron House.

It was a terrifying night for staff and patients at the Royal Infirmary. One bomb struck the Nurses' Hostel in Newport Road but luckily the nurses were all on duty. The same bomb shattered a window while a surgeon was at work in an operating theatre. No-one was injured but the lights went out, and the patient was taken to an adjoining room where the operation was completed by torchlight. Other bombs fell on the chapel, the decontamination unit and a dispensary storeroom containing highly inflammable solvents. As it happened, the Fire Brigade was able to offer instant assistance from its sub-station in the

53.   *Howard Gardens School on 3 March 1941.*

54. *The Carlton Rooms after the raid of 3 March.*

basement of the partially built Maternity Hospital in Glossop Terrace. This basement also served as a shelter for those women patients who were capable of being helped down the steps by the nurses. If that was not possible they were placed on the floor to give some protection. Nevertheless, normal service at the Infirmary ceased for a time and temporarily it became a war casualty clearing station. Several wards were damaged to an extent where they could not be re-opened until after the war. Astonishingly, there were no serious injuries and next day patients were evacuated to other hospitals at Whitchurch, Merthyr and Mountain Ash. In fact, Whitchurch was rapidly converted into an emergency hospital and 100 beds were made available for the duration of the war.

The Blind Institute in Longcross Street was destroyed at the height of the raid, though within 10 weeks blind workers were once again resuming their contribution to the war effort at new premises in City Road. A Catholic sister and 3 girls were buried under the debris in St. German's church hall when it was hit by a high explosive bomb. Their cries led rescuers to 2 badly injured survivors but the nun and the other girl were killed.

At Howard Gardens High School an oil bomb struck the caretaker's house, turning it into a furnace in a matter of minutes. At the same time, incendiary devices fell on the roof of the school and flames spread rapidly through the dry rafters. So many fires were raging in the city that it was 2 hours before the fire brigade arrived. The caretaker and other helpers worked valiantly to quell the flames but could not save the Girls' Department in the upper storey from complete destruction. At the time, the building had the appearance of a raging

55.   *The damaged CWS building in Guildhall Place.*

inferno, so it was all the more remarkable that part of the school was able to re-open within 10 days.

Once again gallant deeds were performed by members of the public. At a dance hall in Roath, women dashed out to help the fire watchers smother a shower of incendiary devices. It was, "a bizarre sight as the women's multi-coloured frocks were revealed in the brilliant light". Nearby, in Richmond Road, Alun Emlyn-Jones and Tudor Griffiths, both members of the Home Guard, noticed the roof of a house on fire. When they entered to give assistance, they discovered the householder had been overcome by smoke. After rescuing him, they filled the stirrup pump with water to fight the fire. As always such situations were not without humour. The lady, far from showing concern about her husband, asked Tudor and Alun to be careful about spilling water as the carpet was almost new.

In the city centre the Carlton Rooms were reduced to charred remains. Before the war the premises had been a favourite rendezvous for tea dances or a game of billiards. While a part of the building was later re-opened as a canteen for British and American servicemen, the damage was too extensive to justify the cost of repair. After the war the site was occupied, first by the British Home Stores, and later by the Queenswest Shopping Centre.

In Charles Street a batch of incendiaries landed on the roof of St. David's Cathedral. The gates around the church were locked and spectators looked on helplessly as the bombs rolled into the guttering and ignited the roof. Eventually members of the church heard the news and received a special blessing from the priest, so that they could go into the burning building and save the Blessed Sacraments.

Once again chaos was caused by delayed action bombs, many of which were dealt with by members of the Home Guard, drawn from the Guest Keen works and Machine Products of Pengam. The readiness of the Home Guard to lend a helping hand during the blitz sometimes had elements of black comedy. When a bomb fell on The Hayes, everyone dropped to the ground except for one new recruit, aged 17, who was blown into a wall by the blast. He was shaken but followed the rest of his company into St. Mary Street where another bomb fell on the CWS warehouse. This time the lad, still refusing to dive for cover, was blown into a telephone kiosk. When asked why he had not tried to protect himself, the youngster replied that he was still waiting for his uniform and had his best trousers on. If he got them dirty his dad would flatten him.

Among the casualties on 3 March was Frank Gaccon who had played rugby for Cardiff and Wales and was the founder of a very successful firm of motor assessors. He volunteered for the AFS before the war began and became its divisional officer. Normally, when the alert was given, Frank drove from his home in Cyncoed to the headquarters in Westgate Street where he and Cliff King, the chief of the regular fire brigade, supervised the demands made on the service. On this night Frank's readiness to lead from the front was to cost him his life. With all the fire engines at full stretch there was a desperate shortage of transport. Frank responded to a call in the Roath area by carrying essential equipment in his car, an American Hudson Terraplane. As he was travelling along Newport Road, a bomb exploded in his path near Summers' Funeral Home. He was killed outright and at first the distorted wreckage of his vehicle was mistaken for the cockpit of an aeroplane. The Chief Constable, James Wilson, paid Frank Gaccon this tribute at his funeral service, "He was as brave a man as ever fought a battle". His sacrifice,

56.   *Frank Gaccon, on far left, with colleagues at Sophia Gardens 1940.*

along with that of other firemen, is remembered at the Fire Station in Adamsdown.

Extracts from the Civil Defence Controller's logbook at the docks reveal some of the drama of this night . . . "Land mine drops on north side of the Roath Dock . . . huge fires reported northwards, evidently the centre of the city . . . police request help for the Blind Institute, Howard Gardens school and Dewi Sant church . . . emergency switchboard out of action . . . police report a plane down in City Road . . . send all appliances available . . . but no appliances to spare".

The following night, schools in Moorland Road and Lansdowne Road were set on fire but not seriously damaged. This time the docks and Penarth were singled out for special attention but, though numerous incendiaries were dropped, prompt action ensured that the raiders had no major fires to guide them to their target. The Mountstuart Dry Dock suffered slight damage and a number of railway wagons, loaded with timber and pit props, were blown up at the Roath Dock. Shipping in the port was unharmed and the most serious incident occurred at Spillers' grain silo, where an incendiary became lodged in the intake gantry and created dust explosions.

Throughout the war, the newspapers of South Wales never missed a single edition but it was sometimes a close call. The Tudor Printing works was damaged in the January raid but the plant and machinery were unharmed. Contingency plans had been made with the other newspapers of South Wales to help each other in a crisis and, after the devastating blitz on Swansea, the *South Wales Post* was printed in Cardiff. On 4 March the *Post* was still being produced in Cardiff

57.   Wyverne Road, where the Palmer Family perished on 29 April 1941.

when, just before midnight, an unexploded bomb fell alongside the *Western Mail* and *Echo* offices in St. Mary Street. There were fears that vibration from the presses might detonate it and both newspapers turned to the *South Wales Argus* in Newport for help. So all the newspapers in South Wales were temporarily

58.   *The effect of a landmine on Coldstream Terrace, 29 April 1941.*

produced in Newport, each carrying virtually the same stories and often the same advertisements. Only the title and headlines were different but all 3 towns had their newspaper, a wonderful example of wartime cooperation in a very competitive business.

The third serious raid on Cardiff took place on 29 April. The most terrifying moments of that night were once again caused by landmines. Altogether, four of them were dropped and the target seems to have been the Civic Centre. Death came without warning for, though the siren had sounded, the German bombers dispensed with their usual prelude of flares and incendiaries. One mine fell harmlessly in the castle grounds but the others had tragic consequences. Two fell on Llanbleddian Gardens and Wyverne Road, killing 23 people. Among them were 10 members of the Palmer family. They had taken cover in their Anderson shelter in Wyverne Road but it offered no protection against the bomb dropping a few yards away.

The other landmine fell on Riverside where several streets suffered extensive damage and 10 more people died. A seaman, who had just come ashore, was returning home to Lewis Street when the mine floated down. As he opened the door, his house was hit and all that was ever recovered from him were the buttons on his jacket. Another resident in Mark Street recalled how the fruit trees were in full blossom at the time but, after the raid, they were reduced to charred stumps.

For those left homeless after an attack there were 67 rest centres in the city, complete with first aid equipment and field kitchens. They should have been opened as soon as the raid began but on this particular night 250 people in Cathays, who had been "bombed out", were left to fend for themselves. They were sent to Gladstone school but, when they arrived, there was no-one to

59.   *The visit of the King and Queen to Canton in March 1941.*

receive them and it was left to the once maligned wardens to give what help they could. At the time this breakdown in communications was kept secret by the ARP Committee as, "disclosure of the facts might affect public confidence".

King George VI and Queen Elizabeth visited victims of the blitz in March. They were given an enthusiastic reception from flagwaving housewives, many of them standing on the ruins of their shattered homes. "The Queen smiled with delight when a female warden presented her with a parcel of 2 silver spoons, tied up with red, white and blue ribbons, as presents for the princesses".

A month later the city received another distinguished visitor. Winston Churchill, always anxious to assess morale for himself, came to Cardiff to inspect the blitzed areas. He was accompanied by his wife and the new American Ambassador, John Winant. Churchill's whereabouts were supposed to be a secret but news of his presence soon spread around the city and the visit turned into a triumphal tour. Onlookers waved Union Jacks and cheered as he promised them, "We'll more than repay them for this". Smoking the familiar cigar, the Prime Minister spent some time at the wrecked Riverside Conservative Club which he had opened 40 years earlier. A framed programme of the opening ceremony was given to him as a gift and he promised to return it to them when the club was rebuilt after the war. At the Royal Infirmary nurses formed a guard of honour for him. The *Echo* reporter noticed that, after the admonishment he had received for not carrying a gas mask during his visit to Swansea, Winston was this time setting a good example to the public. After inspecting Civil Defence units in Cathays Park it was time to depart. As he left he raised his hat with the salute, "Bravo Cardiff! God bless you".

The raids continued throughout 1941 and 1942 but, after the invasion of

60. *Winston Churchill in defiant mood at Cathays Park, 14 April 1941.*

Russia, they were less destructive and less frequent. By 1943 it seemed that the blitz was over but there was to be one final assault from the skies. It came on 18 May 1943 in a raid that lasted only 83 minutes. No more than 50 bombers were involved but they caused widespread destruction. Over 4,000 houses and 140 shops were destroyed or damaged and the lives of 45 people were brought to a sudden end. It was a well planned attack as the enemy first flew north of Cardiff and then followed the railway line from Whitchurch and Rhiwbina into the heart of the city. Matters were made worse because the crews of the anti-aircraft guns were attending a competition in Aldershot and, by the time they were recalled, the raid was over. Cardiff suffered the terror of continental cities as the German aircraft were able to fly at a low level and use their machine guns.

The Luftwaffe was probably searching for the ROF factory when the first bombs fell on Llanishen Reservoir. The factory was unharmed but residents in Birchgrove and the Heath were not so fortunate. Houses in Ton-yr-Ywen Avenue were damaged and 4 people lost their lives when bombs struck their homes in Pantbach Road and Caegwyn Road.

The worst incident occurred when 4 dwelling houses at St. Agnes Road were struck by a landmine. An eye witness graphically described the scene in these words: "From Caerphilly Road one saw the huge column of black smoke rising like a leaping volcano with debris being hurled in all directions". Mr. and Mrs. Ivor Williams and their three small children had taken refuge in their Morrison shelter in the kitchen and this proved to be their salvation. They were able to crawl out of the rubble, but elsewhere rescue parties had to cut and tunnel their way through the chaos until dawn, aware that people were still alive. "One could hear the pitiful cries of the injured. One stricken family was supplied with water,

61.   *St Agnes Road after the raid of 18 May 1943.*

but only when rescuers crawled into a small hole and handed over the water bottle with outstretched hands". Seven people were killed outright by this bomb, either from suffocation or from the impact of the blast on their Anderson shelter. Of the people rescued at the time, two more were to die later from their wounds.

Another stick of bombs fell in Allensbank Road, severely damaging a row of houses and the Heath Hotel. After a landmine fell on Cathays Cemetery, Reta Gale, who lived in Talygarn Street, recalls coming out of the Anderson shelter to find a piece of gravestone from the cemetery on her parents' bed. The graves

62.   *Clearing up after the bombing of Allensbank Road.*

were disturbed to such an extent that dogs were seen next day scampering along Allensbank Road holding bones in their mouths.

Five people, including a nine-year old child evacuated from the Home Counties, died when a bomb hit their house in Penylan Road. Just across the road it was once again a Morrison shelter, which was under the stairs and protected with sandbags, that saved Mrs. Webber and her family. The house had collapsed on them and, "the next thing we knew was that things were cascading down on to the shelter". At first the rescue party saw little hope of finding them alive. Eventually their shouts were heard and their morale was uplifted when their dog, Kim, scrambled into the shelter with them. A flask of coffee was handed through a tiny hole but it was more than 6 hours before they were rescued. Like many, who experienced the terror of the blitz and lived to tell the tale, Mrs. Webber commented, "None of us would ever grumble about anything again".

As the raiders passed over the city centre, 2 firewatchers lost their lives in Charles Street. Not far away, three sisters aged between 4 and 14 were killed in Frederick Street which, at that time, was still a residential area. Major fires erupted at the Adam Street premises of Brown Brothers, the motor cycle dealers, and at the Welsh Cold Stores in Pellett Street. Three platforms at the General Station were temporarily put out of action and, as the raiders continued towards the docks, they ruptured a cable to take the telephone service out of commission. Bute Street station was sufficiently damaged to close it for several days and a high explosive bomb killed 2 men as it struck the ingot stripping building of the Guest Keen steelworks.

As the bombers continued to follow the railway line westwards, they used their machine guns to strafe a munitions train, leaving pockmarks which are still visible on the bridge across Sanatorium Road. They jettisoned their remaining bombs on Canton and one of the last missiles to fall on Cardiff struck 4 terraced houses in York Street. Mr. and Mrs. Schiller and their two daughters lived at number 37. When the raid began, they crawled into their Morrison shelter and pulled the settee in front of it for additional protection, a decision that probably saved their lives. The whistling of the bomb was followed by a crash of bricks and glass as the settee was hurled across the room. Their house was wrecked but the Schiller family were able to clamber out of the wreckage. The bomb had fallen on the house of their neighbours, Mr. and Mrs. Turner. They were killed but, as rescue workers were removing their bodies, Mrs. Schiller asked whether they had found the Turners' daughter, Grace. The rescuers resumed their search and found to their amazement that she had survived under the rubble. Later Grace confirmed that she and her parents had been watching the raid and, when they saw the bomb hurtling towards them, they made a belated, unsuccessful dash for the Anderson shelter. The Schiller family were taken to relatives in Lansdowne Road but Mrs. Schiller and her husband returned to York Street as soon as they could, fearful that looters would start scavenging among the ruins for their belongings.

Charles Hallinan, the Civil Defence Controller, later said that the raid, "was plotted by a Nazi who knew his Cardiff". Was he the notorious Hans Kuhnemann who had systematically spied out the area before the war? There is another theory that the attack was made in revenge for the Dambusters' raid on

63.   Rescuing victims of the blitz.

the Ruhr. This had taken place the previous night and was led by Wing Commander Guy Gibson who had married a girl from Penarth. If this was so, the raid on Cardiff was planned and carried out with breathtaking speed and efficiency. From the German point of view the raid had been a success. Yet the enemy did not escape entirely unscathed as 3 bombers were shot down on the Somerset side of the Bristol Channel.

The Controller was unstinting in his praise of the rescue parties, "who recovered 50 people from under wreckage, 21 of them being brought out alive". As dawn rose, one of the civil defence workers was passing a battered house in Rhydhelig Avenue. To his astonishment, through the broken windows, he heard a piano and voices singing, "I'll walk beside you through this world today". The singers were a young married couple, sending their own message of defiance from amid the destruction around them.

Few people realised it at the time but this was to be the last time bombs would fall on Cardiff. When the Allies over-ran Normandy and Brittany in the summer of 1944, they discovered launching sites for the V1 and V2 terror weapons pointing towards South Wales. The invasion had taken place just in time to save Cardiff and other cities from an even greater ordeal. As it was, no district of the city was left unscathed by the blitz which had destroyed 600 buildings and damaged 30,000 others. The raids on Cardiff were not as severe as those inflicted on Coventry, Plymouth or Swansea, but they had brought premature death to 355 people and serious injury to another 502.

At the height of the blitz, the Chief Constable commented, "The people of Cardiff have upheld a resolute and determined attitude to meet and resist attack from the air with both courage and confidence . . . everybody carried out their duties in true British fashion". Such words may appear quaint in this modern age but nevertheless they are true.

Chapter Five

In Short Supply

Fair Shares For Everyone

More than half of Britain's food was imported before the war and the German U–boat campaign could have reduced the nation to starvation. As it was, though meals might be monotonous with any luxuries at a premium, everyone had enough to eat even when shipping losses were at their worst. Unlike the First World War, when a failure to introduce rationing for 3 years had brought the country close to famine, plans had been made to ensure that food supplies were fairly distributed. On 8 January 1940, every person was required to register with a retailer for their rations of 4 oz. of butter, 12 oz. of sugar and 4 oz. of bacon. Other foodstuffs, including meat, were rationed soon afterwards.

It has been said that the British people ate more healthily in the war than at any time before or since and today's health experts would almost certainly have approved their wartime diet. No more than half a pound of butter and cheese a week ensured a low intake of fat. The sugar ration was always meagre and, from its introduction in July 1942, the allocation of sweets and chocolate never rose above a pound a month. Children may have found this a hardship but their teeth were certainly healthier as a result. Diabetic people were given an increased meat ration but no sugar or sweets. This did not stop suspicious glances in the butcher's shop when a diabetic was given the extra meat.

Bread was not rationed except for a short time after the war in 1946. The "national wheatmeal loaf" was a strange off-white colour which, according to an opinion poll, pleased only 14% of the population. In banning the white loaf to save shipping space, Lord Woolton, the Minister for Food, admitted that the nation preferred white bread, "but I don't believe it wants it at the expense of troop movements".

Other items not subject to rationing were eagerly sought. Fish was always scarce and expensive. Game was usually available only to the wealthy but the popularity of the rabbit increased by leaps and bounds as it could be fricasseed, stewed or made into a pie. Vegetables were never rationed but items such as onions were in short supply. A former greengrocer recalls that he sold a large onion to one customer who was so delighted that she tied a piece of ribbon around it and kept it until Christmas. Supplies of fruit were equally treasured.

64.   *Wasting food was a crime.*

65. *In any weather there was always a queue for fish.*

Bananas disappeared after Christmas 1940 and banana essence added to boiled parsnips tasted nothing like the real thing. There are tales of children who were given this fruit for the first time after the war and tried to bite through the skin.

The most wearisome aspect of wartime austerity was the endless queue. Rumours that fish, rabbits, or a fresh supply of cooking apples had just been delivered to the local shop, soon spread far and wide and hopeful customers quickly formed a line. Sausages, often dubbed "breadcrumbs in battledress" were one means of filling an empty belly and I remember queuing for hours with my mother at Fry's pork butcher's shop in Bridge Street. There was the tension as you neared the shop and wondered if supplies would last until it was your turn. Both Mr. Fry and his assistant exchanged cheerful banter with their customers, which probably helped to keep everyone's sanity, but the sense of relief when we were sold our pound of sausages, definitely no more than that, was unbelievably exhilarating.

To lighten the dreariness of wartime rationing a points system, which was copied from the Germans, allowed individuals to purchase the occasional treat subject to availability. Items in shortest supply required the most points. For example, in May 1942, one person's supply of points for the month could be used to purchase a small tin of salmon and a pound of dried fruit. The majority of people turned down such extravagance in favour of more mundane items such as dried peas, tapioca or spam, the letters of which stood for, "Supply Pressed American Meat". Dried egg was another innovation introduced by the Americans. The egg ration was usually restricted to one a week but a single packet of dried egg was the equivalent of 12 shell eggs, and could be scrambled, made into an omelette, or used to make a cake. George Thomas, a member of the NUT Executive in the war, was once given a present after addressing a meeting in Newcastle. It was a package containing one fresh egg which George carefully carried back to Cardiff. In telling the tale later he said, "It seems laughable now but remember it was wartime and we were all on rations - my egg was an extra treasure".

On the whole rationing was both popular and successful. It created a sense of fairness which helped to bond the nation in its common struggle and ensured that no-one went hungry despite horrendous losses of merchant shipping. Unrationed food was price controlled and there was considerable resentment when it disappeared from the shops. Sometimes it was sold from "under the counter", an accusing phrase directed at shopkeepers who kept choice items out of sight, either for favoured customers or for use in private barter.

Regulations were strictly enforced. The *South Wales Echo* reported in April 1940 that Tom Lewis and Vivian Searle had both been fined for selling food off the ration. Mr. Searle's excuse that he had some bacon left over and was afraid it might be wasted was not accepted and a £2 fine was imposed. Life was far from easy for the grocer or butcher who had to cope with a multitude of Government regulations, some of them patently absurd. After a grocer was fined £5 for overcharging a customer a farthing, a letter to the *Echo* in March 1942 complained about the "existing and ever-increasing rules and orders" of the Ministry of Food. It pointed out that experienced assistants were being called up for National Service and questioned how young replacements could be expected to understand all the intricacies of food rationing and ever changing prices.

One way of stretching the rations was to dine in the works' canteens or at the British Restaurants which were introduced as a cheap way of providing a midday meal for the general public. They were self service cafeterias, operated by local authorities, and were a natural development of the emergency services of the blitz. The title, "British Restaurant", came from the Prime Minister who said, "the public may as well have the name if they cannot get anything else". In fact these canteens offered good value with the average price of a meal about 10d. For that you could have a hotpot, curry, vegetable pie or stew, accompanied by a pudding, bread and butter and tea. The first centre in Cardiff was opened by the Lord Mayor in January 1942 at George Street in Butetown. A dozen more soon followed in other parts of the city but some British Restaurants had their problems in the early days. The quality of food at the Whitchurch centre was criticised in February 1942 after 400 meals had been wasted in a week. Councillor Edgar Chappell argued that, "people could not be expected to buy cold stew day after day". Matters improved soon afterwards but, as another councillor noted, "people must not expect a Ritz meal for 10d". Some customers expected rather more than just their meal and a widespread disappearance of cutlery led to a

CHARGES
2 COURSE DINNER (ADULT)   9
1 COURSE DINNER   "   7
SOUP

CHILD'S 2 COURSE DINNER

DINNER MENU
SCOTCH BROTH
CHOICE OF
BACON SAVOURY
HARICOT MUTTON
VEGETABLE PIE &
SAUCE
CAE   TOE
STEA   DLIV
RICE

66.   *Menu at a British Restaurant.*

warning that, if matters did not improve, people would have to bring their own knives and forks.

Despite restrictions on the menu they could offer, the cafes and restaurants of Cardiff continued to trade. A cup of tea or very weak coffee was available at the Kardomah or Dutch cafes in Queen Street and, even after it was bombed, the Carlton continued to offer afternoon tea accompanied by a trio of musicians.

The Louis in St. Mary Street and the Continental, next to the Capitol cinema, were among other popular restaurants.

Don't you know there's a war on?

Not only food was rationed. When clothes rationing was introduced in June 1941, every person was entitled to 66 coupons a year and, for those unfortunate enough to lose everything in an air raid, an emergency supply of coupons was issued. At that time, 11 coupons were required for a lady's woollen dress and 26 for a man's three-piece suit. Clothes rationing marked the demise of standardised school uniforms and immaculately turned out sports teams until the war was over. By 1945, when the clothing allowance had been reduced to 41 coupons, people had learnt how to improvise. The tails of men's shirts could be cut off to provide extra collars, while shoes were repaired over and over again. Laundry bags were not on ration and, with a little ingenuity, could be converted into ladies' blouses. Originally the head scarf or turban was introduced to protect women's hair against factory machinery but the garment soon became fashionable headgear for all occasions. There was neither the time nor the shampoo to have a regular set or perm.

The utility look was introduced in 1942 with the aim of using the minimum amount of material. For the men, there were fewer pockets, no turn-ups on

67. *The wedding of John and Eileen Watts in February 1943.*

trousers and the double-breasted suit was no more than a prewar memory. Ladies' dresses were made in a smaller range of colours, hemlines were raised and the number of pleats in skirts was reduced. Many of the restrictions proved to be very unpopular and, within two years, most of them were removed. The Bespoke Tailors' Guild announced, "Popular opinion has killed the austerity suit. Nobody liked it".

Wedding dresses were still for sale but required an exorbitant number of coupons. When Eileen Quick married John Watts at St. John's Church in Canton in February 1943, she was fortunate enough to have a large family of aunties and uncles. Everyone rallied around with coupons to ensure that the bride had a white wedding. The bridesmaids' dresses were all borrowed and passed on from one wedding to the next. Eileen's relations pleaded with their butchers to provide brawn, tongue and a ham for the wedding breakfast. The happy couple were even lucky enough to have a wedding cake, courtesy of their baker. Such actions indicate the kindness to be found in a closely knit community at that time.

When we remember how oil tankers were a prime target for German submarines, it is not surprising that petrol was in desperately short supply and was one of the earliest items to be rationed. For a time every motorist was entitled to a basic allowance, depending on the horsepower of the car, which for a small Austin was four gallons a month. Supplementary coupons were

68. *Jay's Salvage Sale 1941.*

issued only for special needs and these ranged from business use to a "Help your Neighbour" scheme. This was a Government sponsored design which in effect encouraged hitchhiking by urging motorists to fill any empty seats. A bag of coal gas, fitted to the roof of the car, was one method of eking out the tiny petrol allocation, though the wary also strapped a bicycle to their vehicle in case they ran out of fuel. In 1942 the basic ration for private motoring was withdrawn altogether.

Coal was the main form of heating the home in those days and, while it was not on the ration, stocks were always limited. Householders were urged to share a fire or sift the ashes for lumps of coal which could be used again. They were told to use hot water sparingly and anyone who exceeded 5 inches of water for his bath was considered to be unpatriotic. A Government measure, ordering clocks to be put forward an hour, was introduced as a means of saving fuel. In June, "double summertime" ensured daylight until 11 o'clock at night.

Stores such as James Howell's or David Morgan's were a sad imitation of pre-war days, particularly in winter when the only sign visible in the blackout was the one indicating that the shop was open. The most basic products, even if they were not rationed, were difficult to obtain and the problem of replacing furniture became ever more acute, especially when the blitz began. Jay's Furnishing in St. Mary Street attracted large crowds when it offered war damaged goods in a salvage sale after the raid of 2 January 1941. A year later utility furniture, standardised and fixed in price, became available to victims of enemy action but otherwise supplies were limited to couples about to set up home for the first time or families expecting a child. "Utility production" applied to virtually all household goods. Crockery was plain white and at one stage cups were made without handles. There was just a single standard of quality for pots and pans, sheets and blankets, and electrical appliances.

When the war ended, the electrical department at Howell's consisted of two shelves, mainly stocked with one-bar electric fires and irons. Household items, such as a hot water bottle or a vacuum flask, could only be replaced on production of a medical certificate or proof that the old one was broken. In January 1943, after a serious fire had destroyed the main centre for the manufacturing of parachutes and barrage balloons at Elliott's factory on the East Dock, a section of Howell's store was commandeered to ensure that production was not interrupted.

The longer the war went on, the more difficult it was to obtain good quality children's toys. As Christmas approached in 1944, the *Echo* reported that parents were buying more toys than before the war but they were expensive and shoddy. Manufacturers claimed they could not produce a quality product when the maximum price they could charge was 10/-. The typical present for children ranged from a box of rough coloured wooden bricks costing 9/3d, to a set of small cardboard dolls' faces priced at 1/11d. Many parents preferred to look for home-made gifts in the Christmas bazaars. They were reasonably priced and, while somewhat amateurish in appearance, they were more likely to withstand rough handling. Not surprisingly, the *Echo* reflected that the luckiest children that Christmas would be those receiving toys donated by the people of the United States.

69.   *Keeping up appearances in wartime.*

Second hand goods were always in great demand. The "For Sale" column in the Press was scanned for such bargains as, "Wartime pram, as new, £6" or, "Unsorted military boots, nearly all repairable - no coupons". In an attempt to prevent exploitation the Board of Trade controlled prices for second-hand goods, especially furniture, but it was not easy to apply regulations to private sales.

Women had to find enterprising new ways of displaying their charms as perfumes and make-up were extremely scarce. Substitutes, such as burnt cork in place of mascara, or bicarbonate of soda instead of talcum powder, were the fashion. A face cream could be made out of a mixture of broken egg shells, a few drops of oil and the top of the milk. Stockings, on coupons of course, were restricted to flesh colour or American tan. Laddered stockings were painstakingly mended and in the last resort ladies painted their legs with gravy browning, suntan lotion or some similar concoction and then drew seams down the back with an eyebrow pencil.

Cigarettes, especially the favourite brands, were invariably sold under the counter. It was not unusual for pubs to run out of beer before closing time and landlords often requested customers to bring their own glasses. Whisky and other spirits were expensive and almost unobtainable. Shortages and frustration spread into every field of human activity. If anyone complained, they were given the stock answer, "Don't you know there's a war on?"

Nor was there much chance of taking a break from the war. As there were so few private cars on the road, public transport was strained to the limit. People were asked not to use buses or trains except for essential purposes and another of those accusing posters demanded, "Is your journey really necessary"? People were asked to stay at home for their holidays and, if they ignored this advice, they could expect long delays in reaching their destination. Priority was given to essential traffic.

70.   PAYE on the Cardiff trolley buses 1942.

The Cardiff trams performed noble service in carrying people about their daily tasks, though many of them were in a dilapidated state by the end of the war. The Council intended to replace them with trolley buses which were first seen on the streets of the city in 1942. Trams and trolley buses had the advantage that they did not use petrol though they could cause chaos when they came off their overhanging cables. Travelling was simplified by the introduction on 1 March 1942 of a "Pay as you enter" scheme at a flat rate of 1d for any journey in the city.

71. *A warning to the black marketeer.*

The Black Market

A black market in virtually every kind of merchandise was inevitable at a time of shortages but it never operated on a scale large enough to create serious unrest. If someone could obtain half a dozen eggs, a little extra bacon or some torch batteries at a reasonable price with no questions asked, it would take a strong character to refuse the offer. "Wheeler-dealing" or bartering, where a butcher might have an arrangement with his grocer to hand over extra meat in exchange for butter or sugar, was not unusual and farmers or smallholders might have similar arrangements. Much more serious were the rackets involving fraud or downright pilfering.

Petrol was one of the most sought after commodities on the Black Market.

When petrol for purposes of pleasure was no longer available, most private motorists laid up their cars until happier times returned, but there were always some who tried to evade the regulations and obtain the precious fuel on the black market. Petrol for commercial purposes was dyed red to prevent illegal use but this did not prevent enterprising motorists from straining it through a gas mask to remove the colour. One local man, who worked for a corn and hay merchant, ran a profitable sideline with a few farmers in the Vale of Glamorgan. He collected his grain from the farms but, underneath the sacks in his lorry, he then drove away with a few drums of petrol which should have been used for agricultural purposes.

One of Tom Holdsworth's investigations brought to light a scandal involving petrol coupons. After the coupons had been cancelled with a rubber stamp they were sent from Cardiff to a paper mill in Bristol for destruction. Thieves succeeded in stealing a batch of these coupons and, after carefully removing all traces of the rubber stamp, the villains sold them to be used again. Holdsworth does not indicate whether the thieves were caught but they took a grave risk as Ivor Novello, the famous West End producer from Cardiff, discovered rather unluckily to his cost in April 1944.

The pride and joy of Ivor's life was his Rolls-Royce. A stagestruck female admirer by the name of Dora Constable assured him that he could lease the car to her firm and still use it at weekends. However, the lady in question had no authority to make the offer and Ivor was arrested for contravening the wartime regulations. His plea that he had no idea the law was being broken may well have been true but nonetheless he was sentenced to a month's imprisonment in Wormwood Scrubs. It was a devastating experience for such a sensitive man. Even an old admirer, Winston Churchill, felt Novello was harshly treated but the sentence was almost certainly intended to act as a deterrent to others.

There were several instances of sharp practice involving food supplies. One Cardiff store catering manager worked out a scheme which provided him with 56 pounds of butter for his personal use every 2 months. He submitted one set of figures showing how many meals had been served to his employers, and another more inflated record to the Ministry of Food. Eventually his creative accounting was discovered by the head of the store.

Another racket involved the theft of the emergency coupons issued to merchant seamen on leave. These could be tendered to any butcher in the city, who was then able to use them for fresh supplies. At one stage there were enough emergency coupons passing around Cardiff to feed half the merchant navy. The coupons should have been guarded prior to pulping at Treforest, but slack supervision allowed workers to remove them and sell them at 1/6d a time. People from Pontypridd and the valleys flocked to Cardiff to buy extra meat and nearly wrecked the rationing system in the city until they were caught.

Later there were complaints about wasting money following a report that new hinges were being fastened to the doors of meat lorries. In fact this was a response to criminals who had reached new levels of ingenuity. Meat lorries had a seal on their locks but were still reaching their destinations with some of the cargo missing. Thieves had unscrewed the door hinges without disturbing the seals as they stole the meat.

72. *Ivor Novello.*

The arrival of the Americans brought new opportunities for those dabbling in the black market. A labourer, who stole 12 six-pound tins of American chopped ham, was sentenced to 3 years penal servitude at Cardiff Assizes in 1942. A dubious profit could sometimes be made without resorting to theft. In August 1944 two lorry drivers were fined £20 each for selling 2,000 cigarettes they had purchased cheaply from US sailors. The Treasury had lost £12 in duty on this transaction alone but the *Echo* headline, "Trafficking in US cigarettes Rife in Cardiff" suggests that this case was merely the tip of the iceberg.

A tailor landed in trouble when he purchased some rolls of stolen cloth. Eventually the thieves were caught and implicated him in their confession. A raid on the tailor's home and shop uncovered an Aladdin's cave of rationed goods. Prison or very stiff fines could be expected by those trying to beat the system. An employee at Elliott's parachute factory ended up in gaol when he flaunted his silk shirt a little too obviously and it turned out that he had stolen 9 rolls of parachute silk. When a Cardiff clothier from Richmond Road supplied a mackintosh and trousers without coupons at Gloucester market, he was fined £50 and his customer £20.

Sadly, a minority of dock workers everywhere gained a reputation for thieving practices and Cardiff was no exception. Goods destined for the forces and military hospitals were stolen and the worst incident of all occurred when dry dock workers stripped a ship's lifeboats of their emergency rations. Fortunately the theft was discovered before the ship sailed. Holdsworth claimed it was impossible to prosecute the thieves because no-one would give evidence. He was told bluntly, "Not likely. If it ever came out that I had split, one day there would be an accident, a crane slipping its load, or a case might fall from a ship, and that would be the end of me". When Ministry of Food inspectors were sent to investigate cases of pilfering, the dockers threatened to strike unless they were instantly removed.

73.   *Harvesting in Bute Park.*

Waging War on Waste

While the men of the Merchant Navy risked their lives every day to carry food, raw materials and weapons across the high seas, every household was expected to salvage anything which could be used for the war effort. "Wage war on waste" was a slogan of the Electricity Council but it applied to virtually any item that could be recycled. Bottles and jars, tins, rags and paper were all emptied into different bins and collected. Rabbit fluff was spun into wool and old sweaters were unravelled and then re-knitted.

It was a criminal offence to waste food and what could not be eaten was put into a bin for pig swill. People were subjected to such exhortations as, "Are you eating as much as you need, or as much as you like? If so, eat less and cook potatoes in their skins. Let's have the shipping space instead". In 1942 a Cardiff lady, who used bread to feed the birds, was fined 20/- and told she should have put it in the bin for pig swill.

Every square metre of open land was used to its full potential, as the desperate need to grow as much food as possible took the British people back to their rural past. Bute Park was transformed into acres of waving corn as harvesting became an annual event under the battlements of the ancient castle. Cardiff's parks and golf courses were turned into allotments or market gardens, while the flower beds outside the City Hall were replaced with rows of carrots, potatoes and cabbages. Vegetables replaced flowers as an adornment on top of the Anderson shelter and even bombed sites became temporary allotments. If a home owner did not possess a garden, he was offered free advice on the growing of tomatoes or onions in tubs, window boxes or grass verges.

Every available pair of hands was called upon to gather in the harvest. Boys from the Cardiff senior schools and students from University College went to join the Land Army on the farms of Glamorgan. They were lodged in village institutes, received pocket money, and not only made their contribution to feeding the nation but enjoyed a healthy working holiday at the same time. For many years, even after the war had ended, helping on the land became an extension of the school curriculum and it was not unknown for the games afternoon to be replaced with gardening. Monkton House was one school which sent its pupils to a farm in Lisvane one afternoon every week to harvest hay, wheat, potatoes and other crops. In some country districts, children collected wool from hedges and, after spinning and dyeing it, went on to acquire the skills of knitting garments.

People from every walk of life discovered horticultural skills they never knew they possessed. Not only were keen gardeners prepared to "dig for victory" but, under the guidance of the Ministry of Food, they also mastered the intricacies of keeping pigs, rabbits, poultry and bees. An exhibition in Cathays Park in September 1943 included films and a "Brains Trust" offering advice on all these matters.

Ted Chamberlain's parents were members of a pig club and kept the animal in their garden. When it was ready for slaughtering, this task was carried out under the supervision of a Ministry of Food inspector. The Ministry retained a percentage of the meat and shared the rest with the pig owners. As Mr. and Mrs.

DIG FOR VICTORY EXHIBITION

THE ASSEMBLY ROOM CITY HALL, CARDIFF

SEPTEMBER 8th, 9th, and 10th, 1943

PROGRAMME

Admission Free

74.   *"Dig for Victory Exhibition" at the City Hall in 1943.*

Chamberlain also raised chickens, they were given coupons for poultry feed but in return they had to surrender their egg ration.

Food weeks and Kitchen Front exhibitions were organised by the Ministry of Food. At Howell's store, in September 1940, cookery demonstrations were provided by the Cardiff Gas, Lighting and Coke Company and advice was offered on the best ways of storing food. Drusilla Gaccon, now Mrs. Elliott, was a pupil at Cardiff High School when she was selected to give a demonstration of wartime cookery at the City Hall. She had the very difficult task of making meatless sausages out of a mixture of chopped beetroot, mashed potato and breadcrumbs. Without an egg to bind the concoction together it proved an almost impossible task. Nevertheless, wartime rationing made a lasting impression on Mrs. Elliott because, like so many others, she still regards the wasting of food as a cardinal sin.

There was plenty of advice offering ingenious ideas for the dining table. It was not always acceptable or even practical but many of the suggestions did help to brighten up a monotonous diet. Electricity showrooms issued recipes for such delicacies as bread soup, mock plum pudding or emergency pudding. The latter was a concoction of old mashed biscuits and orange peel boiled to a paste and served with condensed milk. Mrs. Webb's *Wartime Cookery* gave tips on how to economise with fuel, or how to make chutney and pickles enliven an otherwise boring meal.

The nutritional qualities of the humble potato were frequently stressed, especially when it was cooked in its skin, and Potato Pete became a well-known cartoon character whose jingles suggested how potatoes could be enjoyed in all kinds of ways:

> *Potatoes new, potatoes old,*
> *Potato in a salad cold,*
> *Potatoes baked or mashed or fried*
> *Potatoes whole, potatoes pied*
> *Enjoy them all, including chips,*
> *Remembering spuds don't come in ships.*

Likewise, Dr. Carrot promised that he could not only add "sweetness to your savouries", but he could also make you see better in the blackout. Incidentally the Germans believed this myth and ordered Luftwaffe pilots to eat raw carrots to improve their eyesight.

Since there were few consumer goods in the shops, the emphasis was on saving money which would not only help to win the war but could provide a nest egg for a brighter future. Every school and most places of work sold saving stamps and in case anyone needed reminding, the ugly Squanderbug, daubed with the hated Swastika, rammed home the importance of thrift in every possible way. Savings weeks were organised on behalf of all the armed services, during which special events were held to bring colour to the drabness of everyday life.

"Lending to the Limit" was the slogan for Warships Week in January 1942. The programme kicked off with a football match between the RAF and the Army at Ninian Park and ended with a rugby match between Cardiff and the Royal Naval Engineering College. The social highlight of the week was the Warship Week Ball at the City Hall, "which will be as brilliant as wartime circumstances (and coupon rationing) will permit". An exhibition of model ships was displayed

75. *The Squanderbug.*

at the National Museum. Among them were replicas of the *Bounty*, the *Golden Hind* and a working model of HMS *Antelope*, able to fire its guns and torpedoes. To add a little spice, Cardiff was promised it could adopt the cruiser bearing its name if the city raised £1½ million. An indicator in Kingsway kept a tally of the contributions which eventually exceeded well over £4 million.

The last air raid on Cardiff coincided with "Wings for Victory" week in May 1943. The National Museum presented a display which not only showed pride in the achievements of the RAF, but also persuaded people to put their savings towards aircraft production. The highlight of an ATC exhibition in the basement

76. Blenheim Bomber displayed at the City Hall in "Wings for Victory Week".

of Howell's store was a Link trainer, "in which members of the public can experience the thrill of blind flying". On the final day Wing Commander Guy Gibson, hero of the Dambusters' raid, was greeted by an enthusiastic crowd in Kingsway, where the indicator board showed that the city had reached its goal of £3 million.

In 1944 "Salute the Soldier" Week took place at a timely moment. A target of £300,000 was set for Whitchurch, Lisvane and the other country districts around Cardiff. The Rural District's poster, showing a British soldier about to liberate Western Europe, struck the right note for the time and the required sum was raised without difficulty. "Salute the Soldier" week in Cardiff happened to coincide with the Allied landings in France and the city once again surpassed its target of £3 million with ease. Eventually it was calculated that, on average, each Cardiff citizen contributed £18 to the fund. An American baseball match on the Arms Park was one of the attractions of the week but the highlight came on 10 June, when the Welsh Regiment paraded before a huge crowd after being awarded the freedom of the city.

Local causes were not forgotten and one which caught the public's imagination was the fund to repair the blitzed wards at Cardiff Royal Infirmary. Money poured in from individual subscribers and all manner of fund-raising events. Workers at Guest Keen and Nettlefold's sent £250 while a dance at the City Hall raised £100. Some of the smaller contributions make interesting reading. The swear box from International Alloys raised £2 while a young boy sent 27/- by selling his toys. Such gestures demonstrate that this was truly a people's war.

THE LIBERATOR

CARDIFF RURAL DISTRICT

SALUTE the SOLDIER

WEEK APRIL 29th—MAY 6th

● Target - £300,000

77.   *Cardiff Rural Districts salute the Soldier.*

Chapter Six

Making the best of a Long Hard Trail

Disruption of the Family

There were times when it seemed the war would never end. Virtually every home in the country faced upheaval as fathers, sons and daughters could be away for several years. Evacuation to escape the worst of the bombing often proved to be a traumatic experience for parents and children alike. For those who lost a loved one in battle or in the blitz, the scars would never heal and only slightly easier to bear was the knowledge that a father or son was a prisoner of war.

The greatest fear for every woman, who had a man on active service, was the dreaded knock of the telegram boy. One lady told me, "When I saw the telegram boy coming up the path my heart stopped beating for a moment. When I read that it was Christmas greetings from my brother, I was both relieved and angry because of the fright he gave me". Ivor Turner of Newport was only 14 years old when he had the distressing duty of bringing the news that a husband or son had been killed in action. Knowing the contents of such a telegram, he often enlisted the help of a neighbour in giving support to the grieving family. "Many a time I cycled back to the office choked, when I realised the numbing tragedy a family had just suffered". There might be hope of a reprieve if a combatant was "posted missing" but sometimes the uncertainty merely prolonged the agony.

Warrant Officer Frank Jones from Lewis Street in Canton was flying his thirteenth mission over Germany on 14 January 1944. It proved to be unlucky thirteen. Returning from a raid on Brunswick, his Lancaster bomber was shot down near Hanover. Frank, a wireless operator and air gunner, was killed with other members of the crew. The telegram bearing the grim news, "missing, presumed killed", was delivered to his wife, Winifred. She and Frank had been married less than three years and in that time she had seen him for no more than a few months. Their son, Malcolm, was just two years old. A few years ago he made a pilgrimage to Hanover to visit the grave of the father he never really knew, one of the 58,000 British and Commonwealth airmen who lost their lives in raids over Nazi Germany and Occupied Europe.

The local newspapers carried news of the casualties every week, each of them bringing grief into someone's home, sometimes in doubly cruel fashion. Henry Morgan of Alfred Street had lost his leg after being torpedoed in the First World War. Early in 1942 he was informed that both his sons, aged 18 and 16, were killed at sea within a few weeks of each other.

Normally the news that a husband or son was a prisoner of war raised the hopes of an eventual reunion, though it might be a long way off. Graham Hale, a Cardiff Rugby three-quarter before the war, was posted as missing in Libya in January 1942. We can imagine the relief of his parents in Cyncoed when, two months later, they received a telegram bearing the news that he was a prisoner of war. Not so encouraging was the knowledge that a loved one was in the hands of the Japanese who were notorious for their barbarous treatment of prisoners.

78. Warrant Officer F.P. Jones.

Children, as well as adults, lost their lives in air raids or suffered injuries which marked them for life. For them the war was a tragedy but some children have happier memories of the war years. Despite the danger, deprivation and upheaval to their lives, they found the war an exciting experience they would never forget. Children watched with interest the construction of pill boxes, the reshuffling of sign posts to confuse the enemy, or the occasional entertainment provided by the Home Guard and the Army in one of their invasion exercises.

BUCKINGHAM PALACE

The Queen and I offer you our heartfelt sympathy in your great sorrow.

We pray that your country's gratitude for a life so nobly given in its service may bring you some measure of consolation.

George R.I

Mrs. F. P. Jones.

79.   *The King's message to Mrs. Jones.*

The day after an air raid, youngsters began to search for shrapnel, blackened incendiary cases or other souvenirs of the blitz. Sometimes such quests ended in tragedy. In January 1941 a thirteen year old boy came across an unexploded bomb near the River Taff. He and his friends carried their souvenir home to Cathays and hid it in an Anderson shelter. A little later the lad was chopping firewood near the shelter when the bomb exploded and he was fatally injured.

Inevitably children's education was affected by the war. The influx of evacuees meant that some schools became so overcrowded they could only work on a rota system. Often there were as many as 50 or 60 pupils to a single class, either because of a shortage of teachers or because of a sudden increase in the number of pupils. Pencils and text books had to be shared while oral lessons often replaced written work owing to a lack of paper. Even in schools which were able to carry on more or less normally, lessons and examinations were interrupted by air raids as children hurried to the shelters. The logbook for Tongwynlais primary school reveals that in September 1940 the children were sent home on 15 occasions when the air raid warning was given. Nor was it easy for pupils or teachers to concentrate on school work when they were tired and dazed the morning after a raid.

Two of Cardiff's grammar schools were seriously damaged as a result of the blitz. The Boys' Department of Canton High School was virtually gutted in January 1941 though the fire Brigade succeeded in saving the Girls' School. The pipe organ, only installed the previous October, was ruined and many children lost books which had been left in their desks over the Christmas holiday. They were almost impossible to replace at that time. One classroom among the wreckage was just about useable but had no lighting or heating. Russell Jones, then a teacher at Canton, remembers boys bringing their own candles to school to shed a little light while they sat their examinations for the Christmas term.

80.   *A mathematics class at work in Rumney Senior School 1943.*

For the time being, the younger boys were moved to Virgil Street School in Sloper Road. The following September arrangements were made to share the premises of the Girls' Department but, for another 8 years, pupils spent much of their school career studying in makeshift accommodation such as Canton Library, Llanover Hall and Salem Chapel. Every effort was made to ensure as little disruption as possible to their education but inevitably opportunities for practical work were limited and lessons were shortened.

It was a similar story at Howard Gardens, where the Girls' Department in particular was largely destroyed on 3 March 1941. Only the new wing, the gymnasium and the cookery centre were still serviceable. Next day an attempt was made to salvage anything useful. A teacher remembers, "It was the little things that were to remain in the memory . . . the key to the Art Room door . . . but no longer any Art Room . . . the showcase containing the School's precious cups reduced to twisted bits of powdery white metal".

Considerable damage was also inflicted on the Boys' School, much of it caused by the hoses of the firemen. Any items which could be salvaged were rescued the next day, but the most heartfelt loss was the bronze war memorial containing the names of 102 pupils who had died in the First World War. Some repair work was carried out before the end of the war and, as Cardiff High School and Heathfield House shared their facilities with the stricken school, pupils were able to continue their education.

Where fathers were away in the forces and mothers were working, it was inevitable that family discipline sometimes broke down. From time to time there were allegations that idle, uncontrolled youths were taking advantage of the blackout to indulge in an orgy of theft, housebreaking and downright vandalism. Letters to the *South Wales Echo* in December 1944 complain of bedlam in some parts of Cardiff on a Sunday night: "Church services were being conducted to a running obligato of catcalls and general rowdyism from outside". Meanwhile trees, bushes and property were being vandalised in the dimly lit streets. There is a familiar ring to the complaint from a councillor in March 1942 that conditions for naughty children at the approved school in Dinas Powis, with its playing fields and swimming baths, were much better than facilities in conventional schools. At the same meeting, the Chief Constable, in pointing out that 11 children had been birched for petty crime in the last twelve months, regretted that more magistrates did not impose this punishment. He said, "One wonders whether the sting of the birch at the proper time would not have a more salutary effect" than sending a boy to an approved school.

Yet, in spite of the abnormal times in which they lived, the majority of children were brought up in a disciplined environment. Older children in particular were encouraged to make their contribution to the war effort by collecting salvage or helping with the harvest. Many boys joined a cadet force while they were still at school. Weekend camps, manoeuvres on open spaces such as Cardiff Golf Course and some basic military training, all helped to prepare them for service life when they reached the age of 18.

81. Sir James Grigg inspects Canton High School cadets in St. Mary Street 1943.

The Evacuees

Boys and girls who were evacuated often suffered an emotional upheaval, but there were others who were fortunate enough to find happiness with good foster parents. On the outbreak of war, South Wales provided a refuge for 20,000 evacuees from London and the Midlands and many of them passed through Cardiff before they were dispersed to the countryside nearby. The Cardiff Rural District Council was responsible for an area which included the Vale of Glamorgan and districts such as Whitchurch, Radyr, Llanedeyrn and St. Fagans, which nowadays are in the city boundaries.

Though their mothers sometimes accompanied them, most evacuated children were placed in the care of foster parents. Tension between evacuees and their hosts was not uncommon in those early days of the Phoney War when the spirit of one nation, united in a common cause, was still being forged. Some foster parents saw their charges as a source of income. One lady took in 5 evacuees but made certain she rationed them to 2 slices of bread and butter for tea with no sugar in any of their drinks. Bath time was taken in a tub with one lot of water providing for all 5 children. One child with unhappy memories maintains, that "being evacuated was a worse experience than living through the blitz". In fact, by January 1940, despite Government warnings to leave them where they were, nine out of ten evacuees had returned home.

When the blitz began in earnest, the exodus from bombed cities resumed once more and this time there was a warmer welcome for the children uprooted from their homes. In the Rhondda valleys, 2,500 youngsters from Greater London alone were placed with local families by the summer of 1940. Often they were

82.   Departure for an uncertain destination.

welcomed by the colliery band. The *Western Mail* reported how well they had adjusted to their new environment and would return as "future ambassadors for Wales". Their teachers commented that some of them were "enjoying a greater measure of home life than ever before". Certainly many of them looked back on their time in the Rhondda with affection and retained the link with their foster parents long after the war. In September 1995 there was a nostalgic reunion in the borough.

The Cardiff Rural District Council, which was caring for more than 2,200 evacuees in February 1941, faced a number of major headaches. Billeting them was just one problem and often they had to be given temporary accommodation in village halls and schoolrooms. Emergency clothing sometimes had to be found for children dispersed in a hurry with little more the clothes on their backs. By February 1944 the situation became easier as the blitz lessened its ferocity and the number of evacuees in the area declined to 223. Then London came under attack from the V1's and V2's and numbers rose once more to the level of 1941.

In 1939 Cardiff was declared a "neutral" zone, neither receiving nor dispatching any evacuees. Later in the war, after the blitz had already struck the city, Cardiff children were sent to safer areas. Dan O'Neill, later a reporter for the *South Wales Echo*, was evacuated from Grangetown to Clydach Vale. He has written about the anxiety and tears of the parents as they parted with their children but he also recalls, that, from his point of view, "it was a glorious escape from routine . . . the greatest, gaudiest holiday of our lives . . . We couldn't wait to start this great adventure . . . We ranged the mountains, we picked blueberries, we annoyed the sheep and the Home Guard who stumbled through the ferns". As their Cardiff accent acquired the lilt of the valleys and they began to teach their hosts the finer points of baseball, they had few problems fitting into the local

83. *The first night away was often spent in temporary accommodation.*

community. It was also reassuring for the evacuated Cardiff children that they were accompanied by friends from the same school and, as they were not far from home, their parents were able to visit them fairly often. Indeed, from his bedroom window, Dan could see the barrage balloons over Cardiff, "glinting silver in the setting sun".

84. Welsh survivors from the City of Benares.

Bill Bowen, another lad from Grangetown who later became Chairman of South Glamorgan County Council, was one of 4 children evacuated to Aberfan. Bill attended Pant Glas school where, a quarter of a century later, a landslide of coal slurry claimed the lives of 144 victims, most of them children. Bill remembers that Aberfan, surrounded by coal mines, was a culture shock to children from Cardiff but he also recalls the kindness he found there. "The people opened up their homes and their hearts to us and we were safe from the bombing". Yet evacuation was not always a safe option. While Bill was staying at Aberfan, 4 people were killed when bombs fell on the neighbouring village of Mount Pleasant.

Some Cardiff children were sent further afield. Gloria Cigman, then an eleven year old Jewish girl, was sent to a farming village in Leicestershire and "learned to eat with relish every single part of a pig, despite my upbringing. Pork, bacon, ham, trotters, head, tail, I loved it all". Two Jewish sisters had a less happy experience. When they refused to go to church with their hosts and tried to explain "we go to the synagogue", they were told to get out and go home.

Adults, who sought a safe haven, discovered to their cost that it was not always the wisest thing to do. Lord Glanely, famous in racing circles and one of the richest shipping magnates in Cardiff, moved to Weston early in the war. He escaped the Cardiff blitz but in 1942, in retaliation for raids by the RAF, the Germans mounted a number of attacks against non–military targets. It was in one of these Baedeker raids, as the Germans called them, that Lord Glanely was killed.

After the fall of France, a number of schemes were proposed with the intention of sending children to Australia, Canada or the United States. Organisations in America, sympathetic to Britain, promised that children from Wales would be placed with foster parents who had a Welsh background. A letter to the *Western Mail* from Richard Dundon of Syracuse, New York was typical. He wrote of "his abiding love for Cardiff", and promised 150 homes for Welsh children who would return "to a victorious Britain, physically and spiritually as British as they are now". Some parents took advantage of these offers but they lost their attraction after two vessels were attacked by U–boats. In the first incident, on 2 September 1940, everyone was saved including a Canton High School girl whose first thought was to rescue her school scarf. Later that month the *City of Benares* was sunk in another U–boat attack. Five Cardiff children, among them two brothers, James and Lewis Came from Grangetown, were among the 83 young people who lost their lives.

Keep smiling through

Amid the tragedy of war, which was never far away, it was essential that people had some time to relax. Long hours at the workplace or in the voluntary services, together with the drudgery of austerity and shortages, might have led to fatigue and a decline in morale. Consequently all aspects of the leisure industry were regarded as vital contributions to the nation's cause. Holidays, even with travel restrictions, became moments to be treasured. Dancing, the cinema, the theatre and sport, albeit on a reduced scale, were obvious forms of amusement, but cultural activities and entertainment provided by the wireless also offered a temporary respite from the war.

As August Bank Holiday approached in 1944, amid rising hopes that victory was not too far away, many people felt the time had come to relax. The *Echo* sternly admonished such complacency. "The war is not over barring the shouting and the bells ringing". While recognising that people needed a rest from the stress of war, the paper urged them to take their holidays at home and avoid straining transport facilities which were required for such essential duties as evacuating families from the VIs now falling on Southern England: "There are no luxuries at the front and holiday travel at the present time is a luxury". The plea seems to have fallen on deaf ears at the Central Station, as trains to the West of England were so crowded that people tried to clamber in through corridor windows.

Miners descended on Trecco Bay at Porthcawl by train, bus, lorry, taxi and bicycle, while some even walked, pushing a handcart with their luggage. Those, looking for extra comfort, hired furniture vans to carry their bedroom suites and lounge chairs. Others were quite happy to camp out with their own tents. Though all the visitors brought their rations with them, there were queues for bread and fresh vegetables and inevitably there were complaints when local pubs ran out of beer.

On Bank Holiday Monday, there were few vehicles on the road to Barry Island but it was crowded with cyclists looking forward to a day at the seaside. Most Cardiff people heeded the plea to stay at home and enjoyed the wide variety of activities prepared for them. An entertaining afternoon was provided by the Birchgrove Allotments Fete and Funfair in Heath Park. There were refreshments and prizes for competitors with all the proceeds going to the Cardiff Royal Infirmary. Another popular attraction, attended by a large crowd, was the Rumney Horse Show. Works' committees organised sports days in Ely, Splott, Fairwater and Butetown, which were not only fun but somehow helped to symbolise the unity of the nation. The residents of Adamsdown and Rumney

85. *Roath Park in wartime.*

held their own Eisteddfod. At Victoria Park and The Heath, it was carnival time and, on that Bank Holiday evening, many of the city parks offered open air dancing.

Most of the time, for those who wanted peace and quiet, the open spaces of Cardiff were a haven of tranquillity. Mingling with the strollers at Roath Park on a sunny day, it was almost possible to forget about the war for a while. A twenty four hour watch was kept over the park and so it was always open. As a result, people could go for a row around the lake as early as 7 o'clock in the morning before they went to work.

Dancing was always a popular activity for young people. There were several ballrooms in Cardiff at that time but in addition there were dances held at the factories or in local community halls. Margaret Leonard remembers going to a "Bob Hop", so called because the entry charge was a shilling, at the Wyverne Hall in Cathays. During the evening there was an air raid and the band had to compete with the thunder of falling bombs and anti-aircraft guns. The orchestra responded by turning up the volume and the dance continued. Two nights before the big raid on Cardiff in 1941, thousands of people were dancing in the New Year with traditional revelry. At the City Hall, 700 guests, among them the Earl and Countess of Plymouth, attended a ball in aid of the Glamorgan County Welfare and Comforts Association.

Girls were often invited to attend dances at local RAF or Army camps and, after the United States entered the war, the GIs were only too happy to teach young ladies the intricacies of the jitterbug. Parents with teenage daughters might not approve of these outings, but it was not easy to be a heavy-handed parent when these same daughters were being conscripted for vital war work.

Sporting fixtures were cancelled at the outbreak of war and the cricket season came to an abrupt conclusion. The authorities feared an air raid would result in horrific casualties among large crowds but, as it became clear that daylight attacks were not imminent, it was decided to lift the ban on football matches, subject to wartime restrictions. Thus Cardiff City were able to play a friendly match against Arsenal on 13 September 1939. The attendance was limited to 5,000 and each half was confined to 40 minutes so that the crowd could be cleared before the blackout. The City lost the game 4-3, but, as one wag commented, "It takes a blinking war to bring First Division football back to Ninian Park".

The difficulties of travelling in wartime restricted most of Cardiff City's fixtures to friendly matches and competition in the Western Regional League, other members of which included Swansea, Bristol City, Aberaman, Bath City and Lovell's Athletic. Raising a team was not always an easy matter but the club was sometimes able to call on international stars such as Raich Carter, Johnny Carey and Bill Shankley, all of whom served in the area at some stage of the war. In the 1942-43 season, with more and more young players called to arms, the club used a record 72 players for its 30 odd matches.

There were rarely more than 2/3,000 spectators for most wartime matches at Ninian Park but internationals attacted larger crowds. In June 1941 there was a gathering of 20,000 to watch England defeat Wales 3-2. One of the Welsh goals was scored by Billy James, the talented young Cardiff City player. Within a year, he was to become a prisoner of the Japanese and, though he returned and played a few times after the war, his career was terminated by the brutal treatment he received at their hands.

There was a quickening of interest in football when victory beckoned and there was the prospect of a return to normal peacetime activities. With many of their players in reserved occupations, Cardiff City were able to field a more settled side of home grown talent from 1943 onwards. It provided the nucleus of a very successful team after the war and also figured in some interesting wartime matches. When the demands of industry led to an FA ruling that all cup ties had to be played to a finish, a game between Cardiff City and Bristol City in April 1945 lasted 202 minutes before Billy Rees scored the winning goal for Cardiff. In a large crowd of 25,000, some fans went home for tea and returned later to see the end of the game. Seven months later, there was an even bigger attendance for a prestigious fixture against the famous Moscow Dynamo. On this occasion the Bluebirds were unable to field their strongest side and were outplayed to lose 10–1.

86.   *Pre-match courtesies before Cardiff City play Moscow Dynamo, November 1945.*

Wartime rugby followed a similar pattern to soccer. During the Phoney War, crowds of about 5,000 turned up to watch a makeshift Cardiff side, led by Wilfred Wooller, play against Service XVs and those club sides capable of raising a team. In March 1940 a crowd of 40,000 assembled to watch England defeat Wales 18–9, all the proceeds from the match going to the Red Cross. It was the last international to be played at the Arms Park until 1946. When a landmine fell at the River end in January 1941, severely damaging the North Stand, the Welsh Rugby Union were forced to play their wartime internationals elsewhere. It was a severe financial blow as the stand had only been built in 1937 and the Union still owed a considerable sum to pay for it.

Cardiff continued to entertain surprisingly large crowds at the Arms Park though it was several years before the smell of cordite disappeared from the River end. The rigours of war even led to a lifting of the ban on Rugby League players and professionals such as Gus Risman and Jim Sullivan were allowed to take part in charity matches or in games between the armed forces. In recalling those days, Bleddyn Williams says, "It is good to think that in the broken shell that was Cardiff Arms Park we managed to entertain people and bring some cheer into the gloom". On Boxing Day 1945, the North Stand and River end were still out of action when a crowd of 27,000 gathered to watch the match between Cardiff and a New Zealand Services XV. Wilfred Wooller, now safely back home after the horrors of imprisonment at the hands of the Japanese, joined the players in the royal salute before the game.

87.   *Wilfred Wooller salutes the National Anthem at the match between Cardiff and the New Zealand Services, November 1945.*

The cricket ground at the Arms Park became a military training centre but the square was retained for the occasional game. Glamorgan had played only a few wartime fixtures before 1944 but that year the team played 11 matches in South Wales. The most poignant of these was at Cardiff on 12 August when a large crowd assembled to watch the game with the National Fire Service. The match was forgotten as the news spread around the ground that Maurice Turnbull, who had captained Glamorgan and played for England before the war, had been killed a few days earlier in the Battle of Normandy. His great friend and colleague, Johnny Clay, later wrote: "As the crowd stood in respectful silence, perhaps the most imaginative or sentimental among them may have pictured for a fleeting instant the well-known figure out there on the field and derived some small measure of comfort. For Glamorgan were carrying on and he would have wished that".

"Going to the pictures" was the principal form of entertainment for the majority of people and on average they visited the cinema twice a week. In those days Cardiff had 8 large cinemas in the city centre, most of them showing the latest films. Another 11 in the suburbs changed their programme halfway through the week and gave patrons a second chance to see a film they might have missed earlier. However, it took more than a war to open the cinemas in Cardiff on a Sunday. A proposal from the Watch Committee early in 1940 to open them for soldiers in uniform was never implemented because of opposition from the churches. "Sunday was an institution" and allowing cinemas to show films on the Sabbath would be directing the first blow at that institution. It was a view that prevailed until 1952.

When war was declared, cinemas and theatres shut their doors for a week before the Watch Committee decided it was safe for them to re-open. The Capitol began its wartime programmes with *Beau Geste*, starring Gary Cooper, while the Odeon provided lighthearted distraction with *The Mikado*. In the early months of the war, huge crowds queued to watch the Hollywood epic, *Gone with the Wind*. Another American classic was the screen adaptation of Richard Llewellyn's *How Green was my Valley*. The film bore little resemblance to a Welsh mining community but people flocked to see it, even though it was shown during the worst period of the blitz on Cardiff.

War films, fictional or documentary, were intended to boost morale and usually they were well received. *In Which we serve*, starring Noel Coward, was based on Lord Mountbatten's exploits on HMS *Kelly*, while *Desert Victory*, celebrating the turning point of the war at El Alamein, was another box office hit. *Mrs Miniver* was a sentimental but moving Hollywood portrayal of English village life during the Battle of Britain. When it was first shown in Cardiff at the Olympia in October 1942, it was so popular that people were sitting through the performance twice. The management pleaded for patrons to leave after seeing the picture so that the huge queues outside could be admitted. Whatever film was being shown, it was impossible to completely forget the war. The newsreel, shown between the two main features, was for most people the nearest they came to the battle front though, like any other news in wartime, it was subject to censorship.

Music lovers found an excellent alternative to the cinema on Sunday evenings at the Olympia or the Capitol, where the Big Band concerts drew capacity

88. The attractions of the silver screen 1942.

audiences and it was standing room only for late arrivals. Joe Loss, whose signature tune *In the Mood* instantly set the toes tapping, appeared at the Capitol in June 1942. On another occasion the legendary Glen Miller provided a wonderful evening of entertainment for American servicemen and local people alike.

The New Theatre and the Prince of Wales remained open throughout the war to provide live entertainment. In January 1941, Alastair Sim and Leslie Banks were performing in *Cottage to Let* at the Prince of Wales. At the New Theatre a war was not going to stop the annual pantomime. The *Echo* critic, in describing *Humpty Dumpty*, wrote, "Here is enchantment . . . a production which is magnificently staged and admirably dressed"

Local entertainers played their part in upholding wartime morale. In the 1930s Wally Bishop, better known as Waldini, formed a gypsy band decked out in colourful costumes. Their concerts at Roath Park, the Park Hall and other Cardiff theatres always played to packed audiences. When the war began, Waldini formed the Good Companions Concert party and it was not long before the group were recruited for ENSA to entertain the troops. At first they performed at RAF camps but, later in the war, travelled thousands of miles to the Western Desert, Tunisia and Sicily. Waldini often spoke of the tears in the eyes of tough fighting men as Elaine, the vocalist of the band, sang *Where ere you walk* and *Song at Twilight* at the end of the show. His happiest moment came at Catania in 1943 when he met up with his son, recovering in a field hospital after being wounded in action. Later the Concert Party went on to the Far East before returning to Cardiff in time for VE Day. Waldini was a popular figure at Llandudno after the war, where he was often approached and thanked by former soldiers for his part in bringing them a few hours of pleasure in the midst of battle. He died in 1966.

89.   *Waldini's Gypsy Band.*

The midday canteen break, or Workers' Playtime as it was better known, was enlivened with performances from ENSA, works concert parties and dance bands. Local artistes, such as Hilda Banwell and her accordion band, entertained workers at Currans' and other local factories. The Curran Choral Society not only took part in performances at the works but appeared in several public concerts for charity. The group won the Welsh Inter-factory Eisteddfodau twice and participated in BBC programmes on 5 occasions.

The radio, or wireless as it was better known, was not just a means of bringing the war news to the people but also provided entertainment for a huge listening audience. When the Forces' Network was introduced by the BBC in 1941, Vera Lynn soon became known as the "Forces' Sweetheart" with 1,000 letters a week requesting her songs. *Workers' Playtime* remained a popular midday feature long after the war and it was estimated that twice daily broadcasts of *Music While You Work* raised factory production by 15% in the following hour.

Nowadays it is difficult to imagine the enormous popularity of programmes such as *ITMA*. "It's that man again" was the signature tune of the show and Tommy Handley was its lynchpin. He brought together a host of odd characters who gave the nation a variety of catch phrases. "Can I do you now, Sir?" was the cue for Mrs. Mop, the charlady, to join the programme, and "I don't mind if I do" indicated the readiness of the ever inebriated Colonel Chinstrap to accept another drink. The show came to the New Theatre in August 1944 but there was some disappointment that Tommy Handley did not make a personal appearance.

Comics were a great source of entertainment for children and those of us now in our sixties recall the *Dandy* with Addy and Hermy, alias Hitler and

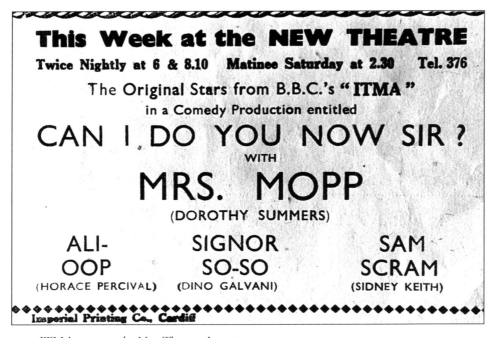

90. ITMA comes to the New Theatre, August 1944.

Goering, the Nasty Nazis. Alternatively there were the heroic deeds of Rockfist Rogan in the *Wizard*, who could shoot down a dozen German aircraft before tea and then win the RAF Boxing Championship in the evening. *The Radio Fun*, in which the stars of Radio constantly irritated the Germans, was another of the best selling children's comics.

It has often been said that people living in the war years, never knowing what the future held, lived their lives more intensely than they would ever have believed possible in the tranquil days of peace. Public libraries were patronised as never before and the *South Wales Echo*, reporting on the preparations for Christmas in 1944, commented on the heavy demand for library books over the festive season. The thirst for knowledge and culture is reflected in the attendances at classical concerts and art galleries, or the popularity of wireless programmes such as "The Brains Trust".

The National Museum of Wales, despite a shortage of staff, offered its services to the public throughout the war. Evacuees and troops based in the region were able to visit the museum and learn about the geography, history and culture of the land which had temporarily adopted them. The staff also gave lectures at Army and RAF camps within a reasonable distance of Cardiff. Most of the finer exhibits were stored away safely but these limitations were counterbalanced by the number and range of temporary exhibitions held between 1939 and 1945.

The majority of these very popular productions related to the war. Ministry of Information films on a variety of topics were well attended and in July 1942 "The RAF in Action" exhibition drew a crowd of 82,000 visitors. The following year the Stalingrad Sword of Honour, specially designed to recognise the heroic defenders of that city, was displayed for two days at the museum. More than 30,000 people queued to see this beautifully crafted instrument which the Prime Minister later presented to Marshal Stalin at the Tehran Conference.

A presentation in 1943, promoted by the Board of Trade, extolled the virtues of utility furniture. In the same year the museum organised its own display, "Fuel and making the most of it", as part of a propaganda campaign to emphasise measures for saving fuel during this period of national crisis. Acquisitions from the Tate Gallery, posters depicting Welsh life and a display of animal photographs offered nostalgic memories of a more peaceful era. It is also worth noting that some of the temporary exhibitions were sponsored by the Council for the Encouragement of Music and the Arts, a body which was later to become the Arts Council.

In November 1944 David Morgan's store displayed the work of the army's educational service. Under the title, "Pursuits of Peace", it set out to show the activities carried out by men and women in their spare time on anti-aircraft sites around Cardiff. As the perils of the blitz receded, the batteries became busy educational centres, offering quizzes, debates, talks on current affairs, art and drama classes, and handicraft clubs. Officers worked alongside gunners in craft work ranging from pottery, dressmaking and carpentry, to the production of slippers and soft toys for children in hospital. Originally it was a scheme intended to lift "Blackout Blues" but for some servicemen it became the preparation for a peacetime hobby or career.

Chapter Seven

The Path to Victory

The Foreign Invasion

Cardiff had an even more cosmopolitan appearance than usual during the Second World War. Its people gave a warm welcome to the refugees and soldiers from every Allied nation but it was natural that men and women, far away from home, should seek the comradeship of their fellow countrymen. The British Council, standing at the corner of Caroline Street and St. Mary Street, provided a common meeting place for all nationalities, whether it was organising cultural events, meeting local people or receiving representatives from their governments.

In time many of these exiles formed their own societies. In April 1942 an Anglo-Belgian club was opened in James Street for the benefit of Belgian servicemen and refugees who had fled to Britain in 1940. Representatives of the Belgian Government were present at the opening ceremony to express their appreciation to the citizens of Cardiff for the kindness given to their kinsmen in their hour of need.

Clement Spiridion, a Polish dentist in Windsor Place, took the lead in forming an Anglo-Polish society. The Polish soldiers, very flamboyant in their swirling cloaks and jackboots, had many talented musicians in their ranks and performed a number of concerts at the Reardon-Smith Lecture Theatre. In 1945, when it became clear that their country was destined to become a satellite of the Soviet Union, many Polish servicemen decided not to go home but instead chose freedom among the people of South Wales.

Those Frenchmen, who responded to General de Gaulle's appeal to fight on after the fall of France, were supported by a number of organisations in Cardiff. The "Friends of Free France" met at 36 Park Place, where one of the activities was to knit and sew a regular supply of comfortable clothing for distribution to the French forces. Two restaurants in Cardiff offered a Gallic atmosphere to French merchant seamen when they were on shore leave. One was above the Pavilion cinema in St. Mary Street. The other was the Foyer des Marins in Newport Road, hosted by Margarite Enderlin and her father, both of whom had escaped from France in 1940. The celebrations at the Foyer were particularly joyful on Bastille Day 1944, just a few weeks after D-Day, when 100 sailors not only enjoyed themselves but at last had a realistic hope their homeland would

5 APRIL-1995

THIS PLAQUE WAS PRESENTED BY

THE SOCIETE FRANCO-ANGLAISE de CARDIFF

WHO OCCUPIED THIS BUILDING FROM 1911-1948

IN MEMORY OF THE FREE FRENCH FORCES

WELCOMED HERE DURING WORLD WAR II

91. *Plaque at 36 Park Place, now the Midland Bank, where the Free French met in the war.*

soon be free. From the fall of France until its liberation, 14 July was set aside as a flag day in Cardiff to raise funds for French people exiled from their native land.

The greatest foreign impact came from the United States. American troops first arrived in Wales early in 1942 when 1,900 men were disembarked at Newport, and in August the first liberty ship, *Artemis Ward*, sailed into Cardiff. These vessels were built along assembly line methods and were mocked by Dr. Goebbels who said, "A ship cannot be bought from a shop window". Events proved him wrong as liberty ships carried men and materials across the Atlantic in a steady stream to prepare for the assault on Hitler's European fortress. It was not long before Cardiff dockers experienced other examples of American ingenuity. The first landing craft, ready for use in the North African campaign, were transported to Cardiff in the *Inveran* in October 1942. Its captain promised that landing craft, each carrying a thousand men, tanks and guns, would soon be crossing the Atlantic under their own power.

By 1943 troop ships were sailing directly into the port of Cardiff and the transatlantic drawl, hitherto associated with Hollywood, became a familiar sound on the streets of the city. In due course US camps were scattered all over South Wales and tangible landmarks of their presence still remain. An American base was established on Whitchurch Common and after the war its garrison planted trees to commemorate their links with the community. At Rhydlafar the 81st US General Military Hospital, still used by the NHS today, was built to accommodate the inevitable casualties when the signal was given to begin the liberation of Europe.

For both Americans and British, the "friendly invasion" was a culture shock. Dockers at Cardiff were not amused when the newcomers called out, "Hey! When do you guys wear your kilts?" Likewise, our knowledge of Americans at that time was restricted to glamorous Hollywood film stars, skyscrapers in New York, gangsters in Chicago and outlaws of the Wild West.

How the Americans were received depended on their behaviour. Inevitably, relationships were not always smooth and there were accusations that the

92.   Arrival of US soldiers at Cardiff 1943.

Americans were, "overfed, overpaid, over sexed and over here". They appeared incredibly wealthy in tired, war-ravaged Britain. Their soldiers wore smart uniforms and were paid five times as much as their British counterparts. Since

93.   Plaque at Whitchurch Common commemorates the American "Invasion".

everything was found for them by the army, their pay was virtually pocket money. Nor was it only money that made them rich. At their supply depot in Barry, they had access to all kinds of luxuries that were virtually a distant memory for most Cardiffians in 1943.

The glamour, the wealth and the generosity of the Yanks attracted female company like a moth to a candle, and it was inevitable there would be romantic liaisons which often led to trouble. Well brought up girls were told not to fraternise with the Americans but others were prepared to offer their charms in exchange for cosmetics, a pair of nylons or some other gift, which these new boy friends seemed able to provide in an inexhaustible supply. No-one knows how many pregnancies were the result of these amorous encounters because, when they occurred, families usually kept the disgrace as quiet as possible. There were exceptions, like the family in Abertillery which celebrated their happy event by flying the Stars and Stripes from the bedroom window.

Racial tension among American troops was another cause of friction and in some places black and white soldiers were not allowed to visit the nearest town on the same night. Even in Cardiff, one of the few places in Britain that had a multi-racial society at that time, there were unsavoury incidents. On one occasion, black GIs were enjoying a cup of coffee in the Silver Lounge in Duke Street when a white officer came in. He ordered the manager to throw them out and was told in no uncertain terms that the policy in this cafe was to treat all customers alike.

When racial clashes erupted in local pubs, it was left to the US military police unit at Llandaff to handle this darker side of the American "occupation". Not surprisingly, many black Americans forged close ties with the people of Butetown where they were given a sympathetic welcome. In fact, some of them, stationed in other parts of the country, spent their leave in Butetown to avoid any hostility from their fellow GIs.

It was also inevitable that, like any army, the Americans attracted their own entourage of camp followers. When 700 black Americans were transferred from Liverpool to Maindy Barracks, the "good time girls" were only a day or two behind them. Tom Holdsworth said, "They looked like savages and behaved like savages". They moved into the area near the quarry on which Maindy Stadium was later built. The footpath separating Gelligaer Street from New Zealand Road soon became known as the notorious BURMA Road ("Be undressed and ready, my angel"). Local residents were appalled at the scenes of debauchery, as naked men and women rolled in the grass or retired to ramshackle shelters of wood and corrugated iron. Despite indignant protests from residents and councillors, the Chief Constable was unable to take any action. American troops came under the jurisdiction of their own military police. As they decided to turn a blind eye to what was happening, there was little the local constabulary could do beyond arresting some of the women on a charge of possessing US Army goods.

Further scandal was created when neighbours discovered that a housewife, whose husband was a chaplain in the forces, was inviting American servicemen and their girl friends into her home. After complaints from neighbours, she was raided by the police and charged with keeping a brothel. In another sordid occurrence, the military police were making a nightly check at Maindy Barracks

94.   American racial attitudes created difficulties at times.

when they found a mother in bed with one soldier and her daughter in bed with his friend. At the time her husband was serving abroad in the British army.

When the US authorities did act, punishment could be severe. Two serious incidents occurred in 1944. An American courtmartial, held at the Cardiff Law

95.   *The "Snowdrop" and the Jeep, both familiar sights in 1944.*

Courts, found a soldier guilty of assaulting an eleven year old child at Maindy Park. He was given 15 years hard labour and a dishonourable discharge. A similar sentence was meted out to a truck driver who had intercourse with a twelve year old girl.

The military police, or "Snowdrops" as they were called after their white helmets, white belts and white truncheons, sometimes meted out their own justice in a manner alien to British eyes. When 20 Americans started a fracas in Queen Street, the Snowdrops tore into them with "truncheons swinging like hammers". Eight of the miscreants were laid out and the rest fled. In another incident, when Bute Street was temporarily declared "off limits" to US servicemen, one black driver ignored the warning sign and set off down the road in his three-ton lorry. As he came out of a cafe he was met by a two man patrol. He panicked, tried to flee, and was shot dead on the spot.

Such incidents should not be allowed to sour the memory of what was generally a warm relationship between the Americans and the people of South Wales, during those years when Britain desperately needed all the allies she could muster. It is a positive image of generous, friendly visitors that remains in the minds of most people. A favourite meeting place for all the armed forces was the Church Army canteen, based at the bombed premises of the Carlton Rooms. Volunteers, who worked there, remember how the Americans would breeze in full of banter and wisecracks but, "They were always charming and offered to help with the washing up".

Some Americans were brash and boastful but this was not true of the majority. Mrs. Owen-Davies of Rumney remembers how a Welsh American, Ralph Williams, who had recently married "and didn't want to waste his money drinking and playing cards", came to tea regularly with his 2 friends. It is just one example of the close links formed between local families and the American servicemen. When they were welcomed into Welsh homes they showed their appreciation by bringing gifts from their PX, a storehouse similar to the British soldier's NAAFI but with far more riches. These could vary from tins of corned beef or pineapples to such scarce household utensil as a frying pan or cutlery. Alun Emlyn-Jones remembers giving a lift to an American officer back to his base. He showed his appreciation in the most practical of ways by removing a large jerry can of petrol from a jeep before placing it in the back of Alun's car.

96.   The US forces were popular with children.

Children were introduced to American comics and the adventures of Bugs Bunny, Superman and Captain Marvel. They learnt to greet American servicemen with the question, "Have you got any gum, Chum?" They were usually rewarded, not only with chewing gum, but Hershey bars and candy as well. Damaged US army supplies were brought to Barry Dock to be destroyed but often the Americans threw tins of food, bars of chocolate and cigarettes to the onlooking children in Gladstone Road. An *Echo* newsboy of those days said, "It may have been broken and battered to them but it was manna from heaven to us". Ted Chamberlain, living near the Glider Field in Llanishen, where the Americans had based a few aircraft, was given a rare treat. He became so friendly with the airmen that one of them took him up for a flight over Cardiff in his Piper Cub aeroplane.

In 1943 sailors aboard an American ship in Cardiff decided to give up their Christmas dinner to a group of pensioners. The traditional meal of turkey, cranberry sauce and all the trimmings was loaded into copper thermos pots and taken to a miners' hall at Aberaman. Fifteen of the crew, who had volunteered as waiters, served and entertained 43 pensioners. When the men returned to their ship, they were too late for their evening meal but not one of them complained.

The following year I was lucky enough to be one of the children invited to a Christmas party at Rhydlafar Hospital. We were given a tea of peaches, spam sandwiches, icecream and orange juice, with a packet of sweets to take home. The afternoon is still one of the treasured memories of my childhood.

While the American influence on our country is more obvious, Welsh culture also made an impression on them. When trains were delayed at Queen Street station, the waiting crowd would sing to keep their spirits up and the Americans loved to listen and join in. An even deeper impression was made on those servicemen, often of Welsh origin, who came to Tabernacl Chapel in The Hayes on a Sunday evening. The magnificent harmony of the congregation often moved these young men, far from home, to tears of emotion.

Close ties sometimes led to marriage and 70,000 GI brides crossed the Atlantic after the war. Living in a strange, new country was too much of a strain for some of the marriages to last but many girls found real happiness with their American husbands. Mary Geib met Richard Bornholdt, an American lieutenant-commander in the navy, when he came to Cardiff in 1943. He was based in Cathedral Road and was responsible for organising the distribution of US stores and equipment. He remained in Cardiff until the end of the war and married Mary in 1944 at the Church of the Resurrection in Ely. Though it was very unusual, she was able to travel to her new home in America before the end of hostilities, leaving her husband to complete his duties in Britain. She had a warm welcome from Richard's family and, when he returned from the war, they settled in California and enjoyed a "wonderful marriage of more than 50 years".

John Marks from Pittsburgh came to Cardiff with the 81st General Hospital Group in 1943. He was stationed at Rhydlafar and never forgot the beauty of South Wales, nor the time, "I came into Cardiff and saw this huge castle in the middle of the main street . . . it was unbelievable . . . like straying into a movie set". John met Beryl Jones from Canton, the lady who was to become his wife, at a dance in the Capitol.

Frank Thompson from Jacksonville, Texas was another serviceman who was based at Rhydlafar and remembered the kindness of the Welsh people towards a boy far from home. His wife, Iris, was in the Women's Land Army when they met. After their marriage they spent 3 years at Jacksonville before Iris's poor health brought the couple back to Bedwas where Frank kept the Church Inn.

At the end of the war 72 girls from Butetown became GI brides. One of these was Rosa Dacruz of Christina Street who married Alfred Holmes from New York in 1947 and enjoyed 35 years of wedded bliss until her husband died. She was one of the GI brides who returned to Cardiff for a reunion in 1982 and there have been a number of further reunions since.

American drive and technology were a new phenomenon to the people of South Wales. The jeep became a familiar sight on our roads and Joan Gregory, a nurse at the time in Llandough Hospital, recalls with gratitude the occasional offer of a lift in an American jeep at a time when public transport was unreliable.

On more than one occasion the Americans showed what they could accomplish when they were in a hurry. Since 1934 the Council had been slowly clearing a site at Temperance Town. When the Americans were allocated the site for a camp, they completed the work in a matter of weeks. Again, after a heavy snowfall in 1944, the council regretted the sale of its solitary snowplough a few years earlier. They were saved from embarrassment when huge US vehicles moved in to clear all the main roads in and around Cardiff.

In June 1944 the majority of Americans disappeared from South Wales as they set forth for the beaches of Normandy with their British and Canadian comrades.

97.   *Farewell from a GI.*

Not all GIs had the opportunity to say farewell to their Welsh friends and fiances. Sometimes only a hasty goodbye message was left and often the strict censorship prevented even that. Some of the GIs kept in touch with their wartime hosts, but others never saw their American friends again and did not know whether they were killed or just forgot to write. Suddenly Cardiff and the Vale seemed a quieter but less exciting place. It was also a sombre reminder of what lay ahead before victory was to be achieved.

D-Day

Preparations for the liberation of Western Europe came to a climax in the first half of 1944 but the planning began more than a year earlier. One Welshman who gathered information vital to the success of Operation Overlord was Aubrey Waters. He was a lieutenant in the Royal Navy, whose unit carried out several covert expeditions into Normandy in 1943 to survey the beaches, map the terrain and take soil samples. Such knowledge was invaluable in assessing the difficulties when disembarking men, vehicles and weapons on a distant shore under heavy fire. Alone in enemy territory, with the darkness their only friend, Aubrey and his crew had to make certain they never left any trace of their visits. If there was any danger of capture, they were instructed to blow up their boat and sacrifice their

98. *Lieutenant Aubrey Waters 1944.*

lives. On D-Day itself, his team was among those to lead the first assault craft towards the beaches. Despite the clamour and carnage of battle all around him Aubrey, who now lives in Llandaff, says he felt much safer among that army of liberation than he had ever felt on those lonely journeys into the unknown a year earlier.

By D-Day, 78% of the supplies for American forces were passing through the docks of South Wales. The ports of Cardiff and Penarth were allotted to the US Army and an American Port Commander was appointed with wide ranging powers. His team included representatives from the British and American armed forces and the various transport authorities. The volume of traffic at the docks was six times its pre-war level and the task of handling it was too much for the dockers alone. As momentum built up for the invasion, units of black and white American troops worked alongside British servicemen to handle the huge flow of men and materials from across the Atlantic.

While spring turned to summer in 1944, huge convoys of vehicles passed through Cardiff on their way to the ports of South Wales. Alan Leonard remembers hundreds of Sherman tanks trundling along Cyncoed Road, turning the surface into a morass that "resembled a ploughed field". Afterwards American soldiers helped council workers to repair the damage caused by their fellow countrymen.

At the end of May the open space on the east side of the Queen Alexandra Dock, known as the "Prairie", began to fill up, with "vessels and craft of infinite variety in an almost unending stream; guns, tanks, vehicles, bombs shells . . . and then, at last, the men themselves". In view of the huge quantities of ammunition spread around the docks, the fire brigade was on full alert in case of an accident or a surprise attack from enemy aircraft.

99.   *The Prairie June 1944.*

To ensure secrecy, as the convoy assembled in the Bristol Channel, the seaside resort of Barry Island was closed for a week. On Friday 2 June the first vessels began to leave port, only to be put on standby next day as bad weather and gales threatened the timing of the invasion. After a 24 hour delay, conditions improved and every ship sailed to the minute, an historic sight for those who were able to see it. On 6 June, just 30 hours after sailing from Cardiff, men and equipment were being unloaded on to the Normandy beaches.

The planning of operations after D-Day was also organised from Cardiff. Units of American servicemen were trained as stevedores so that they could later handle cargoes in France. Once the initial bridgehead was established, thousands of miles of piping for transporting oil, together with materials needed for the

100. US locomotives arrive in Cardiff.

construction of airfields, were shipped from the South Wales ports to the Allied armies on the continent.

Heavy locomotives, carried by special sea trains from the United States, were among the most spectacular arrivals at Cardiff Docks in the two years before the invasion. The first of them arrived in November 1942, each vessel carrying 52 engines, together with their tenders and rolling stock. Heavy shore cranes lifted these giants, each weighing 100 tons, directly on to lines alongside the dock. Initially they were used to replace worn out and damaged British engines but, in the first 5 months of 1944, they were shunted into the sidings of South Wales. After the invasion they were transported to France to replace the engines destroyed by Allied bombing or by the retreating Germans.

Penarth was virtually an American town during the year before D-Day. In November 1943 the dock was converted into a repair base for landing craft of all kinds. Workshops with the most modern machinery, administrative offices, mess quarters and kitchens capable of serving 400 meals an hour, sprang up almost overnight. Everything was in place to repair the vessels damaged in the Normandy landings, but losses proved to be lighter than anticipated and the facilities were never needed. In July, with the Allied bridgehead in France secure, the Americans departed and Penarth returned to its restful calm once more.

In thanking all the port workers of South Wales, Colonel Frank Ross, Chief of Transportation for the US army, said, "Without your help, our task would have been extremely difficult to accomplish". It was a view echoed in June 1946, when General John Lee, Commanding Officer of the American Supply Service for the European Theatre of Operations, brought a message from General Eisenhower. It expressed, "our lasting gratitude for your contribution to victory and the cooperation you gave to the United States forces".

101. Rhydlafar Hospital.

As men with horrific injuries were brought back to hospitals in this country, it was a salutary reminder of the price that had to be paid in liberating Western Europe from Nazi tyranny. Among the casualties were trainloads of wounded American servicemen who were brought to Creigiau station, usually in the early hours of the morning. Volunteer ambulance drivers, many of them women, met the trains and took the injured men to the US hospital at Rhydlafar. It came to the attention of Colonel A.G. Gould, the commander of the hospital, that the drivers, who were unpaid and often out all night in every kind of weather, were unable to obtain any refreshment. He immediately gave instructions that, after completing their duties, they were to be given a hearty American breakfast in the officers' mess.

The Last Winter

Allied successes in the summer and autumn of 1944 raised hopes that the war would soon be over. On 17 September the blackout was replaced by the "dim-out", a halfway house between total darkness and full street lighting. All windows apart from skylights could now be curtained normally except during an air raid. Partial street lighting was reintroduced and driving at night became easier as motorists could once more use their headlights so long as they were dipped. At the same time, fire-watching was abolished except in the South-east of England where the V1s and V2s were creating a new terror.

In October the Home Guard stood down after more than four years service, and two months later a contingent from Cardiff proudly marched through London in a farewell parade to take their final salute from the King. The occasion

102. The Home Guard stands down, October 1944

marked the end of long nights on guard duty but it was also a time for nostalgia. The formation of a Home Guards Association was viewed suspiciously by one anonymous housewife, writing to the *South Wales Echo*, as an excuse to "have a night on the razzle" and avoid duties at home. "Man about Town" in the same newspaper took a less jaundiced view, reminding readers of , "the debt we owe to the volunteers who turned out so readily in our hour of need".

As Christmas approached, optimism that the end was in sight began to fade as Hitler launched his last desperate offensive in the Ardennes. Though the war news gave rise to anxiety, the *Echo* was in a cheerful mood. "South Wales gets the Yuletide Spirit", the paper claimed, as it forecast that this would be the best Christmas of the war. Most people could look forward to a four day break as

Christmas Day fell on a Monday. Apples, oranges and nuts were more plentiful than they had been since 1939, while there was no shortage of holly and mistletoe. Children at the Ely homes were entertained by sailors from the Dominions, who had made toys for them during their time at sea. Christmas cards were expensive and, rather than buy several cards, it was often cheaper to send a single greetings telegram to a family. Shops were filled with people buying last minute presents, even if the quality left a lot to be desired, and St. Mary Street was filled with traffic, reminiscent of a busy Saturday in peacetime.

For a tired nation, the bitter winter of 1945 was one more hardship to bear. While it was overshadowed by even more severe weather conditions two years later, the violent blizzard at the end of January was described by the *Western Mail* as, "one of the most phenomenal snowstorms within living memory". Trains, unable to move, were draped in icicles, houses were almost buried and ice floes drifted along the Taff. Amid 30 degrees of frost and huge snow drifts, work at the docks and in the collieries of South Wales ground to a halt. The storm brought the greatest dislocation of transport services ever seen in Cardiff and outlying districts such as Rhiwbina, where milk and bread supplies were cut off for 2 days, were virtually isolated.

So serious was the crisis that emergency measures, held in reserve in case of invasion, were now implemented by the city food officer. Rationing restrictions were temporarily relaxed and the night shift at a munitions factory were given food and beds so that production could continue. As water supplies were frozen, housewives in Canton melted snow for cooking and washing purposes. Those who struggled to work, returned to homes without heat as coal deliveries were suspended. At the weekend whole families trekked to the nearest coal yard to collect fuel on bikes, in wheel barrows, or anything else that would carry the

103. German prisoners clear the snow of 1945.

precious cargo. Eventually a rapid thaw brought fresh misery in the form of waterlogged roads, burst pipes and slush several inches deep. British and American soldiers worked to clear snow from the streets and at the weekend they were joined by landgirls and volunteers who were paid 1/6d an hour. Italian and German prisoners-of-war were also brought into Cardiff to help in the snow clearing operations, an indication that they were no longer regarded as particularly dangerous.

As the war turned in favour of the Allies, the people of South Wales became more accustomed to the sight of Italian and German prisoners-of-war. It was difficult to dislike the Italians, especially when Italy switched its allegiance to the Allied cause in 1943. They were allowed to work on the land and many of them established friendships with their former enemies. Prisoners from the camp at Cefn Mably worked on the farms of Llanedeyrn and Lisvane. Alan Leonard recalls how they bartered with local people, exchanging the carvings and toys they had made for cigarettes or confectionery. In some instances it was not uncommon for an Italian prisoner to cycle forth from his camp and have Sunday lunch with British friends. Indeed, some of them stayed in Wales after the war and married local girls. A love of music was something the Italians shared with the Welsh people, and Reta Gale remembers planting potatoes in the fields at Bryn Golau one spring evening when she heard the prisoners on the next farm raising their voices in glorious harmony. In 1985 the Italian POW Association showed its appreciation of the treatment they received in Wales by presenting a trophy for competition at the National Eisteddfod.

This kind of relationship was more difficult to establish with the German prisoners who, after all, represented the hated enemy. Mrs. Phyllis Condon recalls that most of the German prisoners at Tair-Onen Forestry Commission were hard working and happy to be out of the conflict but many were fanatical Nazis. In one incident a German prisoner spat at one of the land girls but unluckily for him she spat back with far greater accuracy.

Grenville Burnell had a happier experience when he encountered a German prisoner at a camp on The Heath in 1944. Grenville, then 8 years old, was a pupil at Allensbank School and was walking though the woods with his classmates on the way to Heath Park for a sports afternoon. As he passed the camp, a prisoner beckoned to him and called out: "Kommen si hier". Rather timidly, aware of the stories of what a Nazi might do to a small boy, he approached the man standing on the other side of the fence. The German passed his hand through the wire and gave Grenville a bar of Cadbury's chocolate, something he had not seen for a long time. No doubt there are German children from those days who could tell similar tales about British and American soldiers.

Island Farm, near Bridgend, was used as a base for American troops before D-Day but in 1944 it became a camp for 2,000 German and Italian prisoners. When the first German officers arrived in November, a local observer commented, "Their bearing and swagger were far removed from the popular conception of the cowed and captured prisoner". They refused to carry their own bags from Bridgend station until ordered to do so by the stationmaster. As he was dressed in a frock coat and a peaked cap, adorned with gold braid, they assumed he was a high ranking general and meekly did what they were told.

104. A whimsical view of the Great Escape.

On 11 March 1945, less than two months before the war ended, 67 prisoners tunnelled their way out of the camp. All of them were recaptured in a week but during that time the whole nation was on full alert. Reconnaissance aircraft flew over the countryside of South Wales as police, former home guards and trainee airmen searched the farms and fields below. The majority of prisoners did not get very far and gave themselves up without a struggle. A local woman saw one of them wandering in the street and, when she tapped him on the shoulder, he meekly allowed her to take him back to the camp. Some had joined in the escape from sheer boredom and, after a few days without food in miserable weather, they were quite happy to return to confinement. In fact only 8 prisoners managed to travel outside Glamorgan.

Two of them reached Southampton before they were caught but the four who came closest to success posed as Norwegian engineers. They stole a car and made their way to Cardiff where they became lost in the streets. A train driver gave them directions in return for a lift but at Blakely they ran out of petrol. Then they were spotted by farm workers and the hunt was on. Showing great tenacity, they managed to hide on an ammunition train until they ended up near Birmingham Airport. Hans Harzheim, who could speak English, was able to wander around the airport for 2 hours and selected a suitable aircraft to fly them home. They planned to hi-jack it the following night but at this point their luck ran out. They were cornered by 5 farm workers, armed with shotguns, and escorted back to Bridgend. They remembered their manners sufficiently to send a note of apology to the doctor, whose car they had stolen, with an offer to pay for the petrol.

This incident was something of a rude shock but, as winter turned to spring, it was clear that the war in Europe was nearly over. One of the hit songs of April 1945 was *Coming Home My Darling*, reflecting the hope that the long years of separation, and in some cases captivity, would soon be over. When VE Day arrived, it was a time for special celebrations at Iron Street in Splott. Herbert Barcello, a prisoner-of-war for five years, had marched 800 miles through Germany before he was liberated. He returned home on the morning of VE Day and two hours after his arrival, his brother, Clifford, came in unannounced after serving 3 years with the Eighth Army in the Middle East and Italy.

Herbert Barcello had seen the full horror of Hitler's Germany at first hand on that final march. He remembered especially a small group of Jews, shivering in 35° of frost and clad only in sackcloth, who were massacred by SS guards and left at the roadside. On 18 April John D'Arcy Dawson, war correspondent for the *Western Mail*, reported from Belsen: "Living corpses lay dying from starvation deliberately imposed by the Nazis . . . this is the story of the ultimate example of human cruelty of 60,000 unhappy people of all nationalities condemned to death by slow starvation". The stories from Belsen and the other concentration camps uncovered the atrocities of the Third Reich and the reasons why the Allies had refused to accept anything short of unconditional surrender from the Nazi leaders.

CARTOON · By J. C. WALKER

ALL CLEAR——IN EUROPE

105. *Peace in Europe.*

Chapter Eight

The Lights go on again

Victory In Europe

Early in May came the news of Hitler's suicide and it was clear that the end of hostilities was near. Yet, as The German Government signed the instrument of unconditional surrender at Rheims, the war ended with a whimper rather than a bang. "VE Day is imminent", read the headline of the *Western Mail* on Monday 7 May but the Russians refused to accept that the war was over until an official signing ceremony had taken place in Berlin. Later that evening came the long awaited official announcement that the next two days would be public holidays to celebrate Victory in Europe.

For some time the people of Cardiff had been preparing to celebrate this historic day. Austerity was relaxed, though only for a short time. "Until the end of May, you may buy cotton bunting without coupons, as long as it is red, white or blue and does not cost more than 1/3d a square yard", proclaimed an official announcement. Women took advantage of the offer to hastily make dresses, skirts and even parasols in those colours. The sides of air raid shelters in Cardiff were painted red, white and blue, while flags, banners and streamers began to decorate the streets, many of which still showed the scars of war.

The previous Saturday a crowd of 40,000 had watched Wales play England at Ninian Park. A Raich Carter hat-trick ensured that England won 3-2 but, apart from a few hotheads thrown out of the ground for "wild and boisterous behaviour", few people worried too much about the result. After 5½ desperate years, most people felt it was time to rejoice. The Cardiff cinemas all carried films offering escapism from wartime dreariness and gloom. Flanagan and Allen were starring in their new film, *Dreaming*, at the Park Hall while at the Empire, Merle Oberon and Cornel Wilde appeared in *A Song to Remember*.

On Tuesday 8 May Cardiff presented an unforgettable scene of happiness and merriment. The day had all the cameraderie of the blitz without any of the danger. Pretty girls linked arms with complete strangers and danced the Lambeth Walk, the polka, the conga or any other dance that came to mind. The bells of St. John's Church, which in the dark days of 1940 would have heralded the dreaded invasion, now rang out in celebration of peace. "Bands paraded and in their wake hundreds of joyous people, waving Union Jacks, marched with the spirit of a free

106. VE Day in St. John's Square.

people". At the docks, every vessel was festooned with bunting as their hooters and sirens added to the bedlam. Some enterprising characters had acquired detonators which they placed on the tram lines. Every time a tram passed over them, there was a loud bang and a cloud of smoke. "Every available inch of a passing jeep" was covered with British and American servicemen and women, singing at the top of their voices. Mingling with the crowds were wounded soldiers in their blue uniforms. They were enjoying themselves as well but their presence was a reminder that this day had been won at a terrible cost.

Along Kingsway, a sea of happy faces grew ever larger and "even the trees seemed to smile". The Civil Defence choir entertained more than 50,000 people in Cathays Park as they sang the *Hallelluiah Chorus*. On the lawn outside the City Hall, 500 boys and girls from the schools of Cardiff sang *Jerusalem, Men of Harlech* and other patriotic tunes, culminating in the National Anthems. Then at 3 o'clock came the broadcast message everyone wanted to hear. The indomitable voice of Winston Churchill which, in less happy times, had promised nothing but "blood, tears, toil and sweat," announced, "The German war is therefore over . . . long live the cause of freedom . . . God save the King".

The children's street parties were already under way and went on into the night. Down came the sombre blackout curtains to be fashioned into fancy dress costumes for the children. The sandwiches might consist of no more than spam or dried egg, and fruit salad was probably a mixture of apple and plum, but such staple fare was usually supplemented with treasured luxuries saved for the great day. In Jubilee Street, a sailor on leave brought home 2 bananas, an incredible luxury, and these were raffled to raise funds for the party.

The uninhibited joy of the day was summed up by a Cardiff housewife: "What a day! We gathered together on our bombsite and planned the finest party the children ever remembered. Neighbours pooled their sweet rations. The corner grocer donated his entire stock of fruit and jellies. The men spent the day clearing the site while the local church lent tables and the milkman brought along his cart to act as a platform. That evening 94 children paraded around the streets, carrying lighted candles in jam jars, wearing all manner of weird fancy dress, singing *We'll*

107. City Hall on the afternoon of VE Day.

108. Celebrating VE Day at Railway Street in Splott.

be coming round the Mountain and led by my small son wearing white cricket flannels, a scarlet cummerbund and a scout's hat, beating a drum. In the dusk it was a brave sight never to be forgotten". Most children received a present on VE Day, more often than not a half crown savings stamp, as toys and consumer goods remained in short supply for some time to come.

It was not long before the adults joined in the festivities and a piano or wind–up gramophone was brought forth to accompany the dancing. In one Grangetown street a shopkeeper, who was also a professional ballroom dancer, appeared in full, impeccable evening dress and swept the local ladies into a series of scintillating tangos. Publicans had applied for an extension to licensing hours well in advance and it was an unpopular landlord who did not add his own extension to that. Unfortunately in some places there was a shortage, not only of beer but also of bottles and glasses, which brought proceedings to an end earlier than anticipated. Hancock's Brewery placed an advertisement in the *Echo*. "Please return all your empty flagons, bottles and stoppers to enable us to maintain supplies".

In the gathering dusk the fun went on. In Birchgrove, residents brought what the *Echo* called "highly polished tables" into the street and celebrated with a candlelit supper. Most streets had their own bonfire with an effigy of Hitler on top and, as these were lit, they caused havoc with the tarmac. Generally, this was a day when the authorities turned a blind eye to most human frailties, but the police decided it was time to put in an appearance when someone started a bonfire in the portico of the City Hall. In Flint Street the residents decided to suspend "Hitler" on a wire rope across the road. Unable to reach the dummy, they doused it in petrol and threw a match to set it alight. Fireworks, probably unstable as they were at least 6 years old, made an appearance here and there and it was a miracle that Cardiff did not burn down that night.

A ball was held at the City Hall and afterwards the dancers joined the great crowd waiting outside to watch an event that seemed a distant memory. The building was floodlit and for many, "that was the moment we knew the war was really over". The building was only able to display itself in all its glory for 2 hours from 10 o'clock till midnight and for the 8 and 9 May only. After that it was back to the dim-out, as the need to conserve fuel would last well into the years of peace.

At Barry Island, the lights glittered for the first time in six years as Collins' funfair stayed open until midnight. Many people remember going to Roath Park that night where it seemed, "the World and his wife were there". As the crowd increased, so did the excitement as fairy lights twinkled among the trees and an impromptu dance began around the lake. While the music played and the people rejoiced, geese and ducks, accustomed to the eerie silence of the blackout, added their cackling and screeching to the chorus.

Not everyone was in the mood for celebrating. There were many people who had experienced loss and suffering. For them it was a time of quiet contemplation and remembrance, as even now the *Echo* continued to strike a sombre note with news of fresh casualty lists in the last few days of the war. In the shell of Llandaff Cathedral a short open air service was held in the roofless nave and community singing at Tabernacl Welsh Baptist Church attracted a large congregation. In Butetown the Moslem community held a special service at their mosque in Peel Street, remembering especially the merchant seamen from among them who had given their lives in the war at sea.

The Summer of 1945

Slowly people made the return to normality, aware that the war against Japan was still not won. The Whitsun holiday was a low key affair, possibly because the bad weather restricted outdoor activities but maybe there were still hangovers from VE Day. A horse show at The Heath was attended by 3,000 people and a similar crowd watched Glamorgan's match against the Royal Australian Air Force when it finally got under way on Whit Monday. The Australians went on to win in two days with all proceeds from the match shared between Australian charities and the Maurice Turnbull Memorial Fund.

Early in June, Princess Elizabeth made the first royal visit to Wales since the end of the war in Europe. Her main duty was to attend the camp of the Welsh Guides in her role as Commodore of the Sea Rangers and she was given a tumultuous welcome by 4,000 guides in Cathays Park. In the same month, a captured German U-boat aroused a great deal of interest when it was displayed to the public at the East Dock.

Officially, strife among the political parties was suspended during the war and, if a by-election became necessary, the party holding the seat was not opposed. In

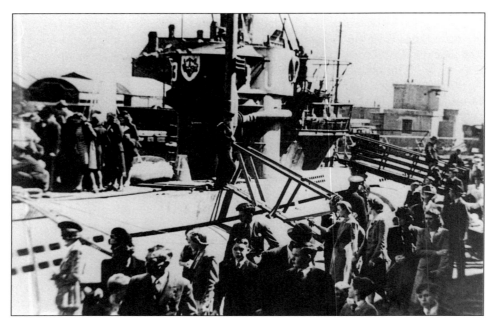

109. Captured U-boat 1023 on display at the East Dock, June 1945.

110. Jim Callaghan on polling day 1945.

April 1942 a by-election was called in Cardiff East when the Conservative member retired. Sir James Grigg, a civil servant invited by Churchill to become Minister for War, stood as a National Candidate backed by the Conservatives and the Liberals. The official Labour party honoured the political truce but there was a contest when Fenner Brockway entered the fray as an Independent Labour candidate. In a low poll Grigg won convincingly and said, "I take it as an overwhelming vote of confidence in the Prime Minister".

At the time he may have been right but it was to be a different story in 1945, when all 3 Cardiff seats fell to the Labour landslide. The wartime coalition broke up soon after hostilities ended and a general election was called for 5 July. In Cardiff, as elsewhere, most people had made up their minds to vote for the party promising a social programme to sweep away the inequalities of the pre-war era. It was a strange election, as service votes had to be collected from all over the world and the results were not declared for three weeks. It was nearly 10 years since people had last elected a government and the *Echo* commented how men and women in their late twenties were ignorant of the voting procedure.

In Cardiff two MPs, who were destined to have outstanding Parliamentary careers, were elected for the first time. James Callaghan was narrowly selected as the Labour candidate for Cardiff South in preference to the Methodist schoolteacher, George Thomas. It was widely believed that Callaghan gained the nomination because of the glamour of his gold-braided naval uniform but George was soon chosen to represent the party in the neighbouring constituency of Cardiff Central. Both men were to be MPs for the next 40 years, but few would have foreseen at the time that Jim Callaghan would one day become Prime Minister and George Thomas would be selected as Speaker of the House of Commons.

That summer families and communities began to welcome home the servicemen who had contributed to the Allied victory. Among them was Geoffrey Booth who had been in the thick of the fighting throughout the conflict. He enlisted just 10 days after the war began and, within a year, he had seen the carnage on the beaches of Dunkirk before he escaped to safety in a fishing boat. Later he served in the Middle East, North Africa and Italy. Now at last he, like many others, was able to enjoy a leave without worrying about a return to possible death or injury.

For some, the war was not yet over. On VE Day a British soldier, on his way to the celebrations in the city centre, passed the American camp near Wood Street and called out, "Hey Yank! Come and have a victory drink with us". The GI, remembering Pearl Harbor, replied, "We ain't got our victory yet. I'll celebrate when we're in Tokyo". It was a salutary reminder that there was still a war to be won in the Far East, where many men from Cardiff were still fighting, or even worse, were prisoners of the Japanese.

The 77th Heavy Artillery Regiment was raised and trained as a territorial unit in Cardiff and was almost like one of the Pals' Battalions of the First World War. The regiment contained many local sportsmen, among them Wilfred Wooller and Les Spence, both legends of Welsh rugby. Billy James, Bob Tobin, Billy Baker and Ernie Curtis, who had won a cup winner's medal with Cardiff City, represented the world of football. The 77th fought courageously as the Japanese over-ran the

111. Margaret and Geoff Booth 1945.

Dutch East Indies early in 1942 but were eventually forced to surrender. For a time the Welshmen were imprisoned on the island of Java but in 1943 they were sent to the notorious Changi Gaol in Singapore. Some of the captives remained at Changi, clearing the jungle with bare hands, while others were forced to work on the notorious Siam-Burma Railway.

112. Welcome home for the prisoners of the Japanese.

Victor Lewis of the *South Wales Echo* sent news of their liberation on 12 September 1945. His report was an account of how the prisoners had written their epic story on six sheets of rice paper, carefully hidden from the Japanese when they made on-the-spot searches. Lewis wrote of the men's three years of hell but also wrote movingly of, "a saga of undying courage and unfailing morale in the face of a battle against disease, ill-treatment and starvation". Their Commanding Officer, Colonel Humphries, said, "their spirit was incredible". All through their captivity they held weekly meetings of the Welsh Society and, "in the filthy night, the songs of Wales would ring out until the whole jungle echoed to *Land of My Fathers* and *Cwm Rhondda*". Many of those who sang would never see their native land again and their comrades made a roll of honour, carved from jungle timber, to remember them.

Some of the Welsh prisoners were sent to Japan, among them Les Spence, once a 14 stone Cardiff forward but reduced to 6 stone by 1945 after two years of toil as a slave labourer in a Japanese coal mine. On 9 August, Les witnessed the blinding flash of the atomic bomb as it fell on Nagasaki, 50 miles away. Years later, as Secretary of the Welsh Rugby Union, he showed the spirit of reconciliation to the manager of the Japanese touring team, Shigi Kono. Les reflected that he owed his life to the atomic bomb and was somewhat surprised to discover Shigi held a similar view since he was training to be a kamikaze pilot at the time.

When they returned home in October, there was a warm welcome for the survivors of the 77th Heavy Artillery Regiment. There were 200 of them, just one in five of the original contingent. The sportsmen among them had mixed fortunes after the war. Their ill-treatment ended the football careers of Billy James and Bob Tobin but Billy Baker enjoyed several successful years with Cardiff

113. Cathays Park on VJ Day.

City. His experiences at the hands of the Japanese turned Wilfred Wooller into a tough, uncompromising cricketer and leader of men and in 1948 he led Glamorgan to their first County Championship.

On 15 August the *Echo* carried the headline, "The World at Peace". The Japanese wept but in Cardiff, as elsewhere in the United Kingdom, joy was unrestrained as the city prepared for another celebration. The City Hall was again the focal point for the festivities but this time there was no floodlighting. Instead drivers switched on their headlights and, as dancing went on till the early hours of the morning, a reporter said the scene was like, "a ballroom on New Year's Eve". Those Americans, who saw Japan as the real enemy, held their own party around the Monument in St. Mary Street, where the statue of Lord Bute was adorned with a top hat. Symbolically the air raid sirens sounded for the last time as they gave the final all clear.

Post-war

The docks at Cardiff, so important in the war, resumed the decline which had begun a quarter of a century earlier. The flow of military traffic ceased within a year or two and those ships, which had used Cardiff during the hostilities, sailed back to their home ports. A final, sombre epitaph to the war took place at Cardiff Docks when a moving tribute was paid to those American servicemen killed in

114. Corner of Croft Street and Rose Street 1998. (See page 53)

action, who were about to be returned to their homeland on the SS *St. Lawrence*. The port began a move back to peacetime activities but coal exports, once the lifeblood of the docks, barely reached a million tons in 1946 and ceased altogether by 1964. The import of apples, oranges and other citrus fruits suggested a return to better days but it would be a long time before the shops discarded the dismal trappings of war. Austerity was to be the companion of the British people for some years to come.

Yet fears of a depression, similar to that after the First World War, proved groundless. At Llanishen, the ROF continued to produce weapons and in 1947 over a thousand people were employed at the factory. Its later involvement in nuclear weapons was to arouse controversy but the plant was not closed until the 1990s. The East Moors steelworks, protected with great care during the war, continued to provide employment until 1978, by which time its plant had become obsolete and annual losses had risen to £15 million. The end of the war led to a number of optimistic proposals, the fulfilment of which are still awaited. One of them was the construction of a Severn Barrage with a hydro-electric plant which would supply, "all our great cities with cheap power".

Many people had been rendered homeless because of the war. Ted and Maureen Thorne had been bombed out on a number of occasions and spent VE Day looking for somewhere to live. Eventually they found temporary accommodation at the US army camp in Cyncoed. The site had no water or electricity but there were compensations. The Americans had departed in haste and left behind unbelievable luxuries of tinned ham, salmon, fruit and even bottles of whisky. The Thornes were later moved to another camp on The Heath but it was not until 1953, by which time they had three children, that they were finally given a house in Ely.

Their dilemma indicates the mammoth task of the construction industry in repairing the ravages of war. Priority was given to the rebuilding of houses. Sometimes they were rebuilt in the same style but it was not always possible to match the original materials. Some streets changed their character entirely, and in many districts of Cardiff there are brick built houses which are a complete contrast with the traditional nineteenth century dwellings of pennant sandstone.

The postwar housing shortage was partly solved by the construction of prefabricated homes. A wooden prototype of one of these "prefabs" was displayed in Wood Street at the end of 1944 and the *Echo* commented, "If the construction is as good as the finish, we shall not have much to grumble about". Made of sheet steel lined with plywood, the standard prefabricated house had a living room, kitchen, bathroom, two bedrooms and a bicycle shed. They were built at a cost of £550 and could be completed in 3 days. By September 1946 contracts were signed to erect them in Rumney, Gabalfa, Caerau and Fairwater. Over a thousand of these houses were eventually built in Cardiff, half of them shipped from America. They were cosy and their lifespan proved to be much longer than was originally thought possible.

Green field sites were needed to fulfil the new housing programmes after the war and Llanrumney was brought into the city boundaries in 1951 for this purpose. However, public opinion forced the council to retreat on one radical idea in 1945 when proposals to build on Llandaff Fields attracted general outrage. Eleanor Thompson, whose family had contributed £5,000 towards the original purchase of the park, reminded councillors that the gift had been given so that

115. *Island Farm 1947.*

116. The memorial to the victims of the blitz in Cathays Cemetery.

the land should be kept, "as an open space for the public and never built upon".

Nearly 15 years were to pass before Llandaff Cathedral was once more returned to its former glory. Generally, the restoration was based on Prichard's work of the nineteenth century but, outside the north door, the opportunity was taken to build a processional way and a memorial chapel dedicated to the Welsh Regiment. The interior of the cathedral was given a lighter, more open appearance though Epstein's statue of Christ in Majesty, looking down on the nave from a new cylindrical organ case, aroused some controversy. Work was finally completed by 1958 and 2 years later a service of thanksgiving was held in the presence of the Queen and the Duke of Edinburgh.

Island Farm, where there had been so much excitement a few months earlier, remained a prisoner-of-war camp for another 3 years. Senior German officers were held there, some of whom were awaiting trial for war crimes. These arrogant Nazis were detested but there were other high ranking officers who won the respect of their guards and people outside the camp. One of these was Field Marshal von Rundstedt, who had commanded German armies in the West and in Russia. He attended church in Bridgend and sometimes took afternoon tea with the vicar. Now that the war was over, restrictions on prisoners' movements were relaxed. They could visit Bridgend and nearby villages where many of them made friends with local people. At the same time they continued to work on farms or helped to bring life back to normal by clearing anti-tank obstacles from the beaches. Many of them were skilled craftsmen who made leather sandals, clothing and children's toys for local people. Old hatreds died to such an extent that 3 of the German prisoners married Welsh brides. The camp closed in 1948 and is now covered by an industrial estate.

People still look back on those six years with mixed feelings. Danger and hardship drew people together and the comradeship of those years is something many will never forget. "There was a wonderful spirit. We all rallied around, whether it was after an air raid or to prepare for a wedding, or just to let the rest of the street know there were oranges in Kennard's". "People were kinder and more considerate than they had ever been before or have been since". Comments of this kind were frequently made to me during the writing of this book.

There was of course a much darker side to life in those wartime years. John Watts was given a 48-hour pass when he married his wife, Eileen, in 1943 and, after a brief honeymoon in London, they did not see each other again for 14 months. Eileen says, "I have always regretted missing the early days of my marriage. Saying goodbye was made worse because you never knew when or if you would see your husband again".

Among those who returned were prisoners-of-war, many of them permanently scarred by their experiences. In many cases loved ones were never seen again. Their bodies lie in foreign fields and under the oceans all around the globe. Since this was a people's war, civilians were not spared and, on the fiftieth anniversary of VE Day, a memorial to the men, women and children of Cardiff who died in the Blitz was unveiled at Cathays Cemetery.

Today, Cardiff is among the most prosperous, thriving cities in the United Kingdom. The ravages of war have long since healed and nearly 60 years have passed since the wail of the siren made us hurry to the shelter, or the sight of a telegram boy set the heart thumping. Every November we remember those who did not live to enjoy the fruits of peace and some still mourn them every day. We can also reflect with pride on a time when the people of our city proved courageous and resolute in the face of adversity. As King George VI said, in a moving tribute when he came to Cardiff in 1941 at the height of the blitz, "'tis not the walls that make a city but the people who live within it".